Crossing Borders

Crossing Borders

Editor
Bruce Kauffman

First Edition

Hidden Brook Press
www.HiddenBrookPress.com
writers@HiddenBrookPress.com

Crossing Borders
Editor – Bruce Kauffman

Cover Design – Richard M. Grove
Cover Photographs – Richard M. Grove
Layout and Design – Richard M. Grove

Typeset in Cambria
Printed and bound in USA

Library and Archives Canada Cataloguing in Publication

Crossing borders / editor Bruce Kauffman.

An anthology of poetry and prose by members of the Canada Cuba
    Literary Alliance.
Text in English.
ISBN 978-1-927725-32-0 (paperback)

1. Canadian poetry (English)--21st century. 2. Short stories,
Canadian (English). 3. Canadian fiction (English)--21st century.
4. Cuban poetry--21st century. 5. Short stories, Cuban. 6. Cuban
fiction--21st century. I. Kauffman, Bruce, editor II. Canada Cuba
Literary Alliance, author

PS8251.1.C76 2015   C810.8'006   C2015-907603-X

Utterance

Sitting over words
very late I have heard a kind of whispered sighing
not far
like a night wind in pines or like the sea in the dark
the echo of everything that has ever
been spoken
still spinning its one syllable
between the earth and silence

W. S. Merwin
from The Rain in the Trees,
(Alfred A Knopf, 1996)

From the CCLA President:

Thank you Bruce Kauffman for being the editor of our 10th Anniversary, CCLA Member Anthology. Thank you to all of the member authors that contributed to this special collection. Thank you to all of our CCLA members for building cultural bridges and crossing borders with us. The mandate of the Canada Cuba Literary Alliance, the CCLA, is to advance cultural solidarity between Canada and Cuba through the creative expression of poetry, prose, art and photography. It is fitting that the title of our 10th Anniversary anthology be called *Crossing Borders*.

As the founding president I started the CCLA in 2004 after travelling to Cuba with my wife Kim. It only took 2 or 3 visits for me to recognize the value of building cultural bridges between our two countries. We have made permanent friendships with both Cubans and Canadians over the past 10 years. We hope you enjoy this fine collection.

Prez Tai / Richard M. Grove

From the Editor:

Following the Canada Cuba Literary Alliance's 10ᵗʰ Anniversary gathering in Cuba in February of 2014, Publisher and President of CCLA, Richard (Tai) Grove came home from with the thought that an anthology honouring CCLA members would be a beautiful way of commemorating the milestone anniversary. When approached by Tai to compile and edit this anthology, I readily agreed and on that day, this anthology was conceived.

Although I was not able to attend what was described by all as a wonderful experience, a number of Cuban and Canadian members were there. While there, many of them created written works of either poetry or prose. In order to, in some way, immortalize the occation, Tai suggested the inclusion of a separate and special section featuring the work produced by those members.

A call for submissions was created and delivered to all CCLA members in late Spring of 2014. Over the course of the next several months, both poetry and prose started making its way across my desk. I was deeply impressed by the well written and self-edited contributions received. Poetry and prose crossing all realms – from observed reflection to grand epiphany, from aspects of love to socio-political wonderings, and from beautiful imagery to wonderful metaphor.

I was, as well, very moved by the poems and stories, and felt in them a 'connection'. Not simply a connection in the words, but of course that was there. It was more a connection to the poets, the authors – to the people themselves. In an association as large as the CCLA is and involving two countries, it's impossible to know everyone. But I felt more and more, as I read through their words, that I grew to know them. With that, I was swept over with an immediate realization of the fallacy of the lines we tend to draw between countries, between people. I could sense the arbitrariness of the separation we often, if not always, create and define as the space between each of us, and as well, the real and yet imaginary lines drawn on a map. It was as if in each of the pieces received – a reaching out, reaching past, reaching through, with word and heart.

You now hold *Crossing Borders* in your hands. You will find in this anthology a very eclectic collection of prose and poems reaching across those perceptual lines of person and place. In each poem or story it is my hope that you too will sense a piece of the person within.

Bruce Kauffman, Editor

Contents

10th Anniversary

Manuel de J. Velázquez León

You Do Not End

Good to find
again and again
that you do not end in your skin,
that your universe continues
in your imagery,
in your smile,
in your laugh,
in your tears,
it continues in me,
inside me,
towards my present and future.

K.V. Skene

No Matter What Sun Warms

in what hemisphere we live
what language
is spoken

we all need a friend

like you
to keep the pulse pumping. The heart
beats till daybreak

when reality slips into focus

and we want to stop the sun
seeing you off
for the last time

loneliness
enters on soft foot,
breath held

as it folds its fine lines around the eyes

and the detritus of older, alternative histories
litter the memory. Only the lucky few
go two by two,

do what they have to do before night
blindness.

Heide Brown

Cuban Beach after the Storm

White waves
rush in rolling rows
towards me

across unnaturally turquoise water
crash onto the sand
suck back quickly
laden with murky spoils

just in time
for the next in line
to rise up
attack
and retreat.

A continual roar.

This I enjoy
through the window
of my warm
dry
room.

Danielle Dinally

The Grip of the Alligator
Inspired by Keyser Manes- a wonderful waiter from Morón, Cuba

I don't know a world outside my own.
I bring over the *Cristal* beer and smile as
my life is questioned. It is you who gives
me life, if you care to look.

The endless days go on, work...and work...
with little time to rest. But as I serve at your request
my smile does not go away. I am still
standing and for what that's worth- I thank
mi Dios-everyday

You say you come here to relax, to take in the sun,
to see our old cars, to try our cigars, to feel that
white sand between your toes. You are given our best.

I receive my own rations, you may have heard.
Paradise, *si*? No-no-
They promise me one thing and give me another.
They pay me in one currency and charge me in another.
They stopped my sister in the streets thinking she's
something she's not...mistaking her beauty.

My smile gets bigger but my eyes...they don't lie.
Here there is no future. I can say it as natural as breathing.
I know...it's normal for you to be amazed at my calmness.
What else can I do?

Any other reaction, I will be chewed and-speet out.
My English is only fair, here we call it the *caimán*.
For you it's just an animal, but for me it's the whole world.
The caimán holds me, tells me how to speak, what to do,
how to live, who to know, who not to know.
It chews my rights, my dreams...everything is swallowed
back down.

My grandmother used to live in its gut as well.
I can show you on the map if you care to look.
She tried to escape. I don't have to tell you
how that turned out.

La verdad-the truth-I am tired of it. There is so much
a person can take. You hear one thing, I know another.
Lies, deception.
The days go on, I continue to serve to survive,
happy as ever. But sometimes I don't want to survive,
I want to live.

I tell you how it really is. There isn't much else.

You must live it to fully understand.

Is not hell, but *is* not heaven.
Cosas no son faciles- things are not easy,
you will hear that a lot here.

John Hamley

Shopping with Miriam

I don't use milk here. It is expensive and I don't feel any need for it—even coffee cooked the Cuban way goes well without it. But today I was in a store with Miriam, with a bag of powdered milk in my hand. Chiqui uses it in her coffee and I had wanted to buy her some.

We had first gone to *La Luz de Yara* where I had wanted to buy some serviettes, but they had run out of serviettes, so after Miriam had bought what she had come for, turkey sausages and a block of cheese, we had walked across the park to this store.

Now I had the bag of milk in my hand and there were serviettes on the other side of the store, but they were on a shelf behind a counter and there was a huge crowd of people in front of that counter, and I would have to line up for a long time to buy them there. And Miriam's legs were getting tired. What should I do? My salesgirl must have read my mind— she suggested that we ask a saleslady who had no customers in front of her to go to pick up a package of serviettes and bring it here, where I could pay for it together with the milk. And that's how we did it.

Actually, it hadn't been serviettes that I had wanted to buy in the first place. What I needed was toilet paper. I had caught a cold and used toilet paper to blow my nose, so much of it that I had brought the house down to its last two rolls. Yesterday a man sitting in a doorway on my street had laughed at my runny nose and teased me, "Ha, ha, you've caught the Cuban *catarro!*"

I would have preferred to use paper napkins. Presumably they have those in Cuba, too, and paper towels also, but I have never seen either. Cubans don't like to waste things and that includes paper. Chiqui cuts her serviettes in the middle, making two out of one.

I had tried to buy more toilet paper but the neighborhood store had run out of it, and so had all the other stores I had tried, even downtown. Chiqui had told me that a store at such-and-such a street corner still had some, but by the time I got there they were out of it, too.

Later that day I would be able to buy some. A truck had come to *La Luz de Yara* with a load of merchandise, including toilet paper, just as Miriam and I had been about to leave, but those goods wouldn't be available for sale until after they had been unloaded and entered into the inventory. I would come back to get my rolls in the afternoon—but I had wanted to buy serviettes now, just in case.

That having been accomplished, Miriam wanted to have a little treat before going back home. Her favorite jello and ice cream place was just a block away so we walked over there, but they hadn't made jellos that morning and were out of ice cream cones. So, we bought chocolate-covered ice cream sticks instead, and sat down and ate them.

I wanted to buy one more thing, a card to go with Dayi's 15th birthday present that Saturday. Since Thursday would be Women's Day and at fifteen Dayi would be counted as a young woman, Miriam and I decided that a card saying *Mujer*, woman, would be appropriate. They sell that kind of cards on a table in front of the main post office, which was no extra distance to walk. So we went that way, but they had run out of *Mujer* cards. I would have to try to find one somewhere else when I came back for the toilet paper. But just in case I couldn't, I picked up a "Happy Anniversary of the Triumph of the Revolution" card to use instead. It has a picture of Cuba's national flower on it.

Hugh Hazelton

Netherworld

up below
above down there
reversed inverse
down-side up
right-side down
daughter of light
son of darkness
solar goddess and
moon god reflection
mother sky ascending to father earth
I hear the creatures of the night stirring
awakening as the daylight fades away
the warm blackness of life
reaching out fertile again as the dark forest exhales
possibilities
no longer tenuous in the white desert glare
following the Southern stars
to the apex of the world
farther and farther up toward
the Arcantic roof of the planet
the circling ocean whirls
along the wings of circumnavigating birds
above even Argentina and Paraguay where
the blossoming tung trees and white orange grove petals
spread spring flowers in September
though the beech leaves of Patagonian trees wither in May
and at the overside of the world
down where the great landmasses are squashed
along the bottom of the globe
sidling along the walksides
obliquely crabscurrying
backwarding forward past
where the ghettoed rich

cry out from within their gates
lamenting from shuttered towers
suspended from beneath balconies as they watch
monuments and generals implode
and the world swirls around their rejection
left above as the others climb
scampering happily downward
to the sharing streets
or run headlong up
toward the waiting earth
in spiralling lowerarchies
moving from right to left
down to up
out and in
and the men wave coquettishly
at the women striding by

Patrick Connors

Reprise

Fluorescent lights
dim perceptions
smiles flash for a moment

clock-watchers
computers warm up
conversation cools

another day has begun
in the sort of place
hoped to be behind me

where truths are discovered
sought for so long:

to be self-contained
as a contemplative

yet ready to be
part of everything

to not give into
idiosyncrasies and insecurities
especially my own...

to love the unlovely
and love the lovable all the more

to work with energy, assertiveness,
and give the world its due
with consistency and integrity.

I am grateful for how
life is entirely different
after 5 PM, before 9 AM.

The conversations are unscripted;
all I want from you
is to know how you are feeling

how your day has been
to share a meal with you
and maybe my latest poem

I am also grateful because
after 9 AM, before 5 PM
I am still the same person.

As if to spite myself
I have finally learned

never to be afraid
to be who I am

how to be alone
but not lonely

to not make trials worse
than they really are

to be aware of where I am
instead of dreaming
where I feel I ought to be

George Arnold

Poolside Vision

December summer day.
Sun squats low overhead.
Pool waters shimmer,
winking an opalescent come-on.
Beneath the surface,
shadow moves nearer,
slender against the pale depths.
Gentle waves are broken.
As she arises from below,
a golden vision emerges.
Dark hair frames and enhances,
the brown skinned beauty.
Sensual lips,
smouldering eyes,
a Polynesian goddess,
appears as from the surf.
Droplets sparkle in the sunlight,
jewels to adorn her beauty.
The countenance of regality.
Slowly she climbs the steps,
emerging from the pool,
a vision in her swimsuit.
She turns and strolls my way.
Her stride is smooth and languid.
My heart beats more strongly,
with her very approach.
Stretched out on my chaise,
I am entranced.
My eyes are riveted,
fixed upon hers,
while she slowly approaches.
As she nears I arise.
Leaden legs lift me,
moments an eternity.
She moves gently into my arms.
Soft flesh presses mine.
Damp bodice chills and enflames.

Tender, moist lips,
graze gently across mine.
Cool dark tresses
caress my cheek and cling.
Gently she sits me back down,
reclines me again in my lounge
Softly she calls my name.
Her voice echoes,
as though down a tunnel,
gradually increasing in volume,
taking on a new clarity.
Senses awaken anew
aware of my surroundings,
of the drink spilled across my chest,
of my soulmate by my side,
though differently clad,
my vision in the flesh.

Yanet Alejo Milian

Legacy from the Time
To my beloved Baracoa

Quiet city
surrounded by mountains
a variety of trees
bird songs in the wind.

Outstanding nature
rich cocoa beans
beautiful snails
paint the scene.

A honey river
touches my feet
soft fruit ripens into
unexplainable feelings.

Coloured flavours
my eyes perceive;
sunrise caresses my cheeks
lonely in the time it hides.

Crystalline creek
next to the street
coconut palm,
bananas, coffee tree.

Supreme beauty
found here
existence merged with the sea
its distinctive emblem.

Island-formed square mountain
at the horizon
a forest bed
of clouds.

Araucanian trails
everywhere
dark and ancient caves
Endemic fashion in the air.

Kimberley Grove

Our Cabin in the Woods

A square wooden box
Hidden in the forest
Snow-buried in the depth of winter
Turns the world inside out
Exchanging city for solitude

Friends doing what they want
Bill snoozing on the couch
Tai and Juli sliding over the snow
In X-country skis

Me, pen in hand
Thawing from the energetic
Walk through 2 ft high walls of snow
Toes just starting to toast

Blackness inside now is solid
Scent of burning cedar
With a small red light of crackling coals
White light outside stretches from land to sky
Windows steamed as if someone had showered

Not even a clock ticks
Silence except for
The gentle syncopation of the fire's
Breathing with Bill's snoring

Such a friend is in this cabin
Not like the dark dingy one
We purchased years ago
Pictures hanging on the wall
Like a little homestead

Warm in a moment of pioneer life

Raymond Fenech

The Boat that Bled

Inside it my youth juggles with the ghosts
frozen in the scent of weather-beaten wood.
Through its gaping crevices
rust oozes from the anchor
bleeding around a fossilized starfish.
Seagulls make a cacophonic melody
as if teasing humans for their limitations;
proud of their natural potential
to fly, float and walk on land.
This time capsule of youth is shattered
by the gasman hooting his horn,
a weekly wakeup call for his customers.
Those summers are now like some forgotten tale
when fresh fish glittered in their armoured scales
and time hung on the fishing line,
sinking into an abyss of green before it could age.
Wet fingers cut easily by nylon thread,
but no blood was ever drawn.
Youth was invincible, I couldn't be hurt.
Now, I am mortal again,
the pain excruciating from being human.

Roger Langen

white flag

grandmother came out waving
a white flag, three little girls
after, like droplets from a leaf
after rain, first two and then one
the soldier killed Souad, 7, first
ringlets under his helmet
orthodox, the news outlets surmised
a settler perhaps, Amal, 2
died minutes after, grandmother survived
but lost her arm

but the BBC liked 4-year-old Samar best
her image bright and pretty, bounced
to Toronto and Sydney and back, intact
video from a Belgian hospital
"they killed my little sister," she said
her smile winning, unmarked
by the wreckage of her spine
a smile, the only defense
a child has

will the unknown soldier suffer, too
will the memory of his two comrades
hurt him, snacking on the tank top
(as reported) as he fired
and will he marry when he returns
will he be a father, too
and if his daughter smiles
will he know
that she is asking him to love her

and oh! did the BBC remember to ask
who it was
picked up the white flag

Tara Kainer

A new poem for Hashem Shabaani

Hashem Shabaani Nejad.
Exotic name & land lyrical,
melodious. Picture
the man on Iranian TV
dark hair blue eyes,
fearless. "Waging war
on Allah", promoting
"Corruption on Earth",
"Threatening National
Security", crimes confessed
after three years in prison &
feet plunged into boiling water

Hashem Shabaani Nejab.
32 years old
Dialogue Institute Founder
Human Rights Defender
Educational & Cultural Organizer
Activist Pacifist
Teacher Father
Husband Son
Critic
of men disappeared
into the night &
arbitrary executions
"Never used a weapon
to fight these atrocious crimes
except the pen," he said

Hashem Shabanni Nejad.
Farsi & Arabic Poet
shaping thoughts smithing
words about Karoun
your beloved River, your
Prison, in languages
outlawed & treacherous

See the photo. Five pairs
Of sandaled feet
Dangling legs clothed to the calf
Chains hanging from shackles
In the background a crowd
Of men snapping pictures

Execution Day

The sky a clear cloudless blue
The colour of your eyes
And in the foreground those
Ten bare feet
Luminous
Amid the blonde sun of Khuzestan
Hashem Shabanni Nejad.

Hashem Shabanni Nejad was an Arab-Ir anian poet and human rights activist charged with several crimes, including waging war on god, sowing corruption on earth, producing propaganda against the Islamic Republic, and acting against national security.

One of Shabanni's odes is Homage to Karoun, Iran's largest river. In another poem he speaks of the blonde sun of Khuzestan. Karoun is also a prison in the south of Iran where Shabanni was jailed in 2011. On January 27th, 2014 Shabaani was transferred to an unknown prison and executed. The Iranian government refused to hand over his body to his family for proper burial.

Shabanni wrote primarily non-political poems, but he wrote Seven Reasons Why I Must Die while in prison and managed to have it smuggled out. It was translated by Marcia Lynx Qualey —

For seven days they shouted at me:
You are waging war on Allah!
Saturday, because you are an Arab!
Sunday, well, you are from Ahvaz!
Monday, remember you are Iranian!
Tuesday, you mock the sacred Revolution!
Wednesday, didn't you raise your voice for others?
Thursday, you're a poet and a bard!
Friday: You're a man, isn't that reason enough to die?

Paulos Ioannou

Woman

I am positive that I have no idea
And certainly do not know
What god had in mind
Creating woman
If indeed he is the one who created her
Which I beg to dispute

There are a lot of theories
But theories are just that
Unproven speculations
Beyond our earthly understandings
To explain why woman was needed
Such a thing of constant light in our hearts
Of air and aroma the flower in the night
The sweet song, the melody in the melancholy
Of the early morning
Perhaps she was born spontaneously
To fulfill the need for peace and beauty
The motherhood of love to stay our hand
Away from the thrall of terror and atrocity
To show us another road a new destiny

Wency Rosales

Guiding a Sea Damaged Boat

The cold rain keeps wet
the lonely streets of my city.
My lost steps take me deep
inside my uncertain past.
Every drop of rain has a meaning
in my body, like your hands
guiding a sea damaged boat
to the nearest harbour
where the sun dries
away the abyss
of our sacred encounter.
And I only have the magic
of your silhouette by my side.

The Caring Embrace of Your Body

Poetry takes us softly
riding to unknown places,
Secret wishes are not hidden anymore.
The exquisite magic of the words
fly over the soft touch of your skin
to the caring embrace of your body
in those stormy days,
to be your pouring rain
the colourful rainbow of your eyes.

Keith Inman

The Stone Polisher

Tall as a rail Paco held his strings of beads
for each gringo on their fine day-beds
in the filtered sun under waving palms, shade
that could cook their skin to corn husk.
A lady with stones for eyes put down
her umbrella drink and reached for a necklace.
She told him that in her country, snow
is sand that melts to water, her eyes opaque
as his Uncle's frozen shrimp. He told her
in his very best English that his father and he
plucked these jewels, he must call them jewels,
from rain worn channels of mountain rivers
above the low hills of their home. He waved his arm
south. His father and he had prized out each
unwashed diamond treasure before it reached
the sea. He swallowed, leaving out the part
about the ditch he was scouring beyond the dump
the day a perfect blue sky became a torrential
downpour from rain in the upper valleys,
that had sent an angry wall of water down
the bank they were working. It gorged him out
in seconds, tried to carry him off with the flailing
lizards but his father had grabbed his arm
and held on to a swinging vine. He was very sore
for weeks, but two days later, returned
with his slinged arm and filled its pocket
with a trove of muddy rocks to polish
like oiled fish in the pan. The pink gringo lady
stood up, scratched the back of her leg
with her other foot, then leaned her long neck
toward him and said she had no money,
could he wait? Her cabana was right over there.
She pointed north. Paco turned and smiled
at his mother in the hard shade beyond the invisible
fence, the flash of a smile in her eyes.

Katharine Beeman

2013, Fifteen years here

Fifteen years
I've lived in this apartment
the Cuban 5 in prison cells.

Fifteen years
seen the neighbor kids
change from toddling three's
to elegant eighteen's.
The 5 haven't seen their children grow
missing tortoise steps and hare leaps.

Fifteen years
time to replace the shaky door
wind whistling windows
warped linoleum and cracked wall;
the next door neighbor, more ambitious – or insane
renovated twice, top to bottom, inside out.
No one's stripped the 5's cells
down to the plumbing and let them out.

Fifteen years
trees shadow now my herbs
my heart, their hearts, our hearts
strive toward their native Cuban sun.

We will prune, uproot, replant the world
to see them free.

June Salmon

Cosmos

A word encompassing
unfathomed bounty,
beauty:
starscape midnight universe
splashed with galactic milk and
red-rimmed planets winking
from positions of mystery. ..
our self-imposed cosmopolitanism
but a snippet of endless space.
Click click precision of
domino events;
infinite worlds operate alone
yet link
aligned by unseen clockwork
or magic...
for magic exists:
just ask Earthlings observing -
seasons' rhythmic ebb and flow,
birth, love, compassion,
ideas flowing to fruition,
peace.
Each cosmic form displays
interprets,
adapts
dependant on its entourage,
surround sound,
place in the universe.
Mysterious,
complexly simple,
magnificent to contemplate,
taking years to decipher,
one look to love.

Miriam E. Vera Delgado

Deep In Thought

So many times,
I walk the streets
Deep in thought;
Like a somnambulist.
I move my lips,
Talking to myself;
And those who see me
What will they say?
Is she crazy
Or is she doped?
I talk to myself
And deep in thought
Walk on the street;
And that's how they
See me.
I look for an answer
To my enigmas;
I look for a way out
From the labyrinth.
So very tired
From so much
Walking;
My sight looks distant;
And deep in thought,
I continue on my feet.

Deborah Panko

In late afternoon

laundry hangs from balconies of scarred brick
cathedrals under renovation in a country still at war

this timeworn city that refuses a coat of paint
home to musicians, lovers who come with the setting sun

to the Malecon, Havana's walkway by the ocean
today rosey-white-grey, the hues of a tri-coloured heron

its waves, a background rhythm to Caribbean chants
pouring into themselves on their journey to shore

and we travelers, as remote as longed-for liberation
served sweet pineapple pizza, chocolate ice cream

a kind of mutual first aid, this shared presence
– breathing life into each other before saying good-bye.

Chris Faiers

Big Al On Point
for Patrick Connors

Barrow by barrow load
Big Al built his special point on Roblin Lake
waterfront sells by the foot
& tho Al & Eurithe wished for a secluded spot
a small space for coffee meditations, well ...
poets can handcraft more than wordy magic

Always resilient (and poor)
this was before fame
Al lugged his barrow loads for weeks & months
planted some soft maples and a few firs
sat back & drank - composed - relaxed
and let Nature do her work for a few decades

Years on I finally found his reclusive retreat
... found Al's grave marker first
made many treks from Marmora to A-burg
to honour Al & his best bud, Milt
But it was years before I finally found
the magic landscape of Al & Eurithe's hand hewn refuge

on the work day last summer
prepping for the inaugural A-frame Open House
I gave myself the pleasant task
of gardening Big Al's special point

on the way in for my restorative chore
I wandered the dirt road for a place to pee
for my little dog Chase & me
and I met a neighbour woman with her young in tow

I asked if she had ever met Al Purdy
as her family cottage is but three doors away
& she replied that Al was almost a recluse
so shy that when she was a teen
eager to see the now famous poet's abode
she and a boyfriend (husband now)
paddled slowly towards Al's point

in the shade of his fully grown arbor
Big Al himself sat in a deck chair
reading perhaps, or composing deathless lines

the People's Poet looked up
saw the canoe of teens approaching
abruptly turned his chair away
back towards the A-frame
and his meditations

in the shallows
blue heron awaits
his old friend

Ernesto Galbán Peramo

And While I Promised
So Many Things

And while I promised so many things,
now I feel how sometimes I slowly bleed
on these bitter rocks
that thrust so deep,
just to know that you leave.

News from the House

The house always carries those pulsations
of those who inhabited it their perfume
and with invisible weeping it's consumed
not to see its spaces shared out.
The house sums up a birth
and in the warm side of this world
its roof, its wall, its profound love
poke its stove, its peace, its breath.
The house has in itself what in the distance
we cannot view in the mirrors
by death's whistling echo
which soon sums us up in a dizzy spell,
then it's sad to see they have believed
that the houses do not harbor our luck.

Brian Mullally

My Favourite Colour

My thoughts are all blue, when I write
Or gaze at the unending view.
Of the azure sky in the light
My thoughts are all blue, when I write
Or stare at star laden night
And search for the moon overdue
My thoughts are all blue, when I write
Or gaze at the unending view.
You can stare 'til you lose your reason
On the hottest mid morn in July
Or the coldest clear day of the season
You can stare 'til you lose your reason
Or compose a multiple deeson
As you search for the end of the sky
You can stare 'til you lose your reason
On the hottest mid morn in July
You can sail the world's oceans forever
I've considered doing it twice
And making it my life's endeavour
You can sail the world's oceans forever
Making loved ones a permanent sever
In pursuit a new paradise
You can sail the world's oceans forever
I've considered doing it twice
My thoughts are all blue, when I start
To grapple with thoughts ever new
While love in her eyes sears my heart
My thoughts are all blue, when I start
To consider my fate if I part
From my children with eyes the same hue
My thoughts are all blue when I start
To grapple with thoughts ever new
My life would be blue, if we part
What else can a poor poet do?
It was hopeless right from the start
My life would be blue, if we part
She's anchored my hopes to her heart
As I gaze at this blue beyond blue
My life would be blue if we part
What else can a poor poet do?

Adela González-Longoria Escalona

I Am Not

I am
Emotionless
An orphan of passion
I have
No smile
No look
No voice
I am
A woman without a face
A woman without a body
A woman without a soul
Your oblivion has taken everything away
I am
Inexistence
Dew
Nothing
I am
Nobody –
I am NOT.

James Deahl

November

During the winter of his years, he occasionally recalled that twelve-year-old boy who would, on lonely autumn weekends, walk through the desolate fields of Dog Hill, wind gusts loosening the terminal leaves from the few scattered trees that grew just below the ridge crest. A boy he hardly knew, indeed, perhaps never knew. Yet, on rare afternoons, there seemed to be little difference between that naïve lad and the white-bearded man walking the Wawanosh Wetlands. And while wetlands were not hills, and the passage of decades had changed much, this was also a Carolinian forest harbouring the same bird and animal species. Most import-antly, November was still and always November, a period of pause prior to the final dying.

Dog Hill had for many years been a sub-division of inexpensive houses. It had gradually become home to different dreams, to different imagined futures. But no matter, all the pages of the book of the future are blank, and have never been other- wise. In fact, it could be that there was no hill, no boy to ramble across it when the wind turned chill; maybe such a scene lived only in the memory of one old man, to eventually die with him. Could it ever be proven? But every year November is certain. Even today, skeletal goldenrods shake as winds sweep over the water, turning the slate sky more grey, the mind ever sharper.

Lisa Makarchuk

Havana

Cobblestones, columns
Clip clops, cock crows and salsa
Enduring, silent shadows

Innocence Abroad

Five in the dock
imprisoned, encaged
isolated, locked down, cooped up
shards of betrayal in check
hopeful that Lady Justice prevails
"All Five guilty on all counts."
Hammer blows against her body politic
Scales topple; body collapses
The eagle flies off the shield
To peck at her bleeding flesh

Charity

rejoices the giver
relieves the receiver
renews the believer

later
it demeans the receiver
diminishes the giver
deludes the believer
debases their dignity
into spiritual poverty

Brian Gordon Sinclair

Hemingway's Hot Havana

Why I live in Cuba (baseball story)

Aside from Jane Mason and aside from my writing, people have asked me why I live in Cuba. They must be *loco*, huh?

(He puts the glass down.)

But, one reason is my home, *Finca Vigia*. It means Lookout Farm. A full ten acres of cool, colonial tile and stucco and a great big fresh water pool, all surrounded with orchids and hibiscus and eighteen different kinds of mangoes.

God I love mangoes! But so did every kid in the little town of San Francisco de Paula and they seemed to think it was open season on my mangoes. They stole so many, there were none left for me. When I asked around, I found out there were no sports for the kids to play. They stole out of boredom. Oh, they'd love to play baseball but they were too poor to afford the equipment. So that's when I decided to sponsor a team. I got them sweaters, hats, gloves, bats and balls and we formed a real team. We named it after my son Gig and we called them the Gigi All Stars. Pretty soon, my favourite automobile had been commandeered as the official team vehicle and I drove them any-place we could scrounge a game. With bats, gloves and nine or ten kids draped over the sides we made quite a sight. And do you know what? I loved every minute of it. By the way, from then on, I got to eat all the mangoes I wanted.

Raúl Vera Delgado

How to Live Without You

The wee hours are the most difficult moment,
when I stretch my arm and I can't find you.
It's like if suddenly time had stopped
and there were no more mornings.
Like if the sun,
ashamed of so much dryness,
didn't want to rise.
In the middle of my sorrow and full of God,
I lift my hand to the heights...
Suddenly, it disappeared amidst a soft mist.
Surprised I brought it back to me...
Where had it gone?
I observed it carefully and...
Oh divine magic!
On the back of the hand lost before,
shone the track of a kiss.
Then I knew we would meet again,
that even though you left,
God had saved you for me in some place,
there, in the unknown...
Then, I could fall asleep.

Donna Langevin

Mariposa

White ginger
butterfly-jasmine
or simply *la mariposa* –
who would guess
despite
your quivering petals
perched
on a long-necked stem
that you're tenacious
as the dandelion
rooting bristly suns
of my northern spring.

Under a heated sky and from
needles of tropical rain
you rocket out of the earth
invade Cuba's parking lots
savannas and fields.

Mariposa mariposa
did your own heart pulse
when warrior-women
hid messages in your leaves
then passed these loaded sheaths
to soldiers on the battlefields
in the wars of independence?

Chosen as the national flower,
purity striping the flag –
mariposa, teach me to
endure all my losses
and the darkness
I carry from childhood.

As I stand here in a rippling
stirred by your scent,
dress me in green and white,
lend me the strength
of your wings.

Bruce Kauffman

noise

the complexity
the complicity

a silence
        is lost
to noise
to movement
to whisper
to a shout
        in the distance
to the yawning
        of the world

we have invented
an alphabet
        to cover the silence

we have invented
machines
        to make that language
        bigger

we have invented
noise

we make it

we lead it

we allow it
        to hide us and

it is only
in the darkness
of night
          alone

and in its silence
that
          we realize and

          we remember

Adonay B. Pérez Luengo

Turtle Dove

In the afternoon, when you come,
you bring quietude with you,
all the peace of the universe.
You are the quiet
and tender turtle dove,
that always comes home
and enjoys the prison of love walls
that we have built.

You Know

You know, my love,
your body smells like ripe plum,
like a morning that bursts sleepily,
like a delayed spring afternoon,
like mango buds and wet soil.

You know, my love,
beautiful is your gesture, your silenced word,
that smile, the denseness of your soul,
your long fingers, your tired look,
the unfinished poetry book and the forgotten date.

Adislenis Castro Ruiz

Peter´s Change

I don´t really know what´s gotten into me these days: every night, right before I slip into my sleep, I wake up frightened.

My heart pounds like a drum inside my chest. I gasp and cough two or three times, and then I fumble in the dark to find the glass of water I always leave on my bedside table. In desperation I gulp down a few sips and fish one pill out of the pack, the one prescribed by the doctor in our last date. I remember his words, "Peter, you must quit smoking".

My heartbeat slowly goes back to normal. I can discern in the shadows – thanks to the dim light filtering in through the window – the painting of Jesus´ Sacred Heart, a gift from my departed Grandmother.

I recall the prayers she taught me when I was still a kid: "Our Father which Art in Heaven...." As I finish, I lean my head on the pillow and sleep soundly all night long.

But tonight is a different one. I don´t know what´s wrong with me. I fumble again for the glass in the dark; but it eludes me. I look around and nothing is familiar to me. I grow desperate again, I don´t know what to do. The painting is no longer hanging from its usual spot, and the dim light coming in through the window is now a searing beam. My eyes are blinded; I can hear a bell and a voice telling me, "Fear not, all is fine. I am the soul collector. I welcome you..."

Paul R. Carr

One vote

Demo-
        Crazy
Is one vote
Per person, except on senior's day
when it's buy one get one free,
We're talking about one vote for the one percent
With supreme court backing
And one percent for the rest
Who believe in freedom, liberty and
Santa Claus

Checking the box
A treatment of botox
Bagel and lox
The Red Sox

If 60 percent vote for a party that gets 39 percent,
Representing less than 25 percent of the total,
Then,
You have,
In Canada,
A Conservative majority,
And quantum physics limits our understanding
of what's happening in the
US and A

For the 40 percent who don't gamble on junk bonds,
They remain ensconced in an oyster-bed,
A solitary group, united and
Larger than the clams that fester

But they are stuck in the outhouse of free choice,
And if you don't vote,
As they say,
Who gives a shit?

James Cockcroft

"¡Daniel vive, carajo!"
("Daniel lives, damn it!")

in memoriam, Daniel Del Solar, d. 13/01/12

You took on the toughest part,
that of dying truly,
said merrily, "Live well, die well."

You died like you lived,
beloved friend,
showering us energy high with love and humour.

In those final days and nights,
as a fire consumes a dry forest,
swiftly, inevitably
you resolved life's needs.

With great sensitivity,
consciousness, reconciliation,
generosity of spirit,
love, above all.

You and Ana united
a singular, awe-inspiring tsunami
of love, and, yes, rage,
gentleness, humour, wisdom.

And, when needed,
the strategic pause…
the bathroom seemed oh so far away.

Dancing the morphine dance, Daniel,
tempered your indignation
at capitalism's spiralling crimes,
with that smile, oh that smile,
of a deeper knowledge,
from which I still learn.

Go then, Daniel, you who
popped new pills, in that final year,
just to ease the pain,
but told few, so you could go on,
helping friends, expecting nothing in return...

Your friends Venezuela, the Cuba Five,
alternative media,
political prisoners,
poets of resistance,
lovers old and new,
Quebec in the South,
CELAC, the *indignados*,
family, Ana, Nina, me...
mother earth, humanity.

You had new waters to traverse,
untested, unknown though fully sensed,
you, Daniel, with Ana,
overflowed them, us, with beauty.

Each day in Montreal,
I touched your and Ana's
last tangible gift to us,
Latino Eyes, photographs
in the wooden box on my desk.

I still do, with neither tears nor dry eyes.
silent now before such beauty.

So I will write,
I will organize,
dance, laugh, garden and swim,
for that is what I do...
and I know you are with me.

¡Daniel vive, carajo!

*

*

The Cuba Five are five Cuban patriots unjustly incarcerated in the United States in 1998 under conditions of psychological torture for having infiltrated anti-Cuba terrorist groups in Miami in order to anticipate and prevent their acts of US-backed terrorism. CELAC is The Community of Latin American and Caribbean States, inaugurated by all the states of the region in December 2012 as an alternative to the Organization of American States — it excludes Canada and the United States.

Jorge Alberto Pérez Hernández

Bad Dream, Good Day

Night of strong breeze,
As usual I'm sitting on the bench to the stern
My clothes wet in the restless waves,
The smell of candle smoke
That mixes with the aroma of a cigar.
My hands are cold
I can see my grandpa´s wrinkled fingers
Fishing lines tied to my feet
A big fish bites the hook
Fear overwhelms me
The fish drags the boat out to the Golf current
A huge wave tilts the boat. It sinks...
Waves bigger and bigger keep coming,
my strength all drained -
Suddenly, from a distance, I hear a sweet song...
"Row, row, row my boat, gently down the stream
Merrily, merrily, merrily, merrily
Life is but a dream..."
What a relief! It is my grandpa
beside my bed telling me:
"Wake up! Wake up! It´s daybreak! Come on!
It´s time to go fishing...!"

June Salmon

Instinct

Trusting instinct a few times in life
I have plunged with reckless abandon
no thought for any moment but the one inhabited;
pure passion
joy
adventure pulled the strings.
Something other propelled me
since the self I knew
was usually humble
timid
hesitant
measuring consequences so carefully
the moments passed
the chance to grasp the golden ring
lost.
Times I let my true self guide
I jumped instinctively
head over heels
through cracks I'd never seen
down roads invisible before
past mountains more magical than plausible.
These are treasured times
nuggets to hold fast
memories precious and unforeseen.
Makes me wonder if I'd found my self before
what life might have been -
or did I need to wait
for wisdom to find me
so I'd trust and know.

George Arnold

Island Queen

In my mind you grace my world
A lovely island queen to worship
Beauty unsurpassed in any dream
With laughter bright on soft brushed lips
Youth still burns in dark brown eyes
Your brown silk skin entices me
Gentles curves heat up my loins
No recourse to fill my need
And still you stand so picturesque
The object of my adoration
I can't get enough of you
Reverence my only choice
Till dreams come true
Till I can fall on bended knee
And show my love in its totality
The love that befits my queen of my heart

Richard M. Grove

In Line for a Permit

"Excuse me. Excuse me, would you mind if I jumped in line before you? It is a bit of an emergency. I have to renew my permit in a hurry."

"Hey buddy, get to the end of the line. We all are in line to get a permit or renew a permit. What makes you so special?"

Dwain looked a bit flush in the face and was now doing a bit of a dance. "Sorry to be a bother but it's my 'Permission to Take a Shit Permit' that I forgot to renew and I'm in a bit of a pickle." Dwain's little dance started to get a bit more animated.

"Ok, ok but next time I might not be so hospitable so just hurry it up."

Gritting his teeth Dwain mumbled a thank you and dashed up to the wicket just as the government clerk with a witches mustache and a wart on her nose slammed her 'Closed, Go to Next Wicket" sign down as Dwain's white-knuckled grip around his permit papers.

"But, but excuse me miss. It will take only a minute. All of my paper work is in order."

"Sorry mister but I take a bathroom break every half hour whether I have to go or not. It's union rules."

By now Dwain was cross eyed. All of the other permit renewal wickets were closed. As if he had a cob of corn jammed up his butt he waddled his way out the front door and ducked behind the first bush he could find.

A half hour later Dwain found himself at the front of the line standing in front of the wart nosed, mustached clerk.

"Next. What can I help you with?"

Dwain stepped forward and said, "I'm here to pay my fine."

"What fine is that sir?"

With a relieved look on Dwain's face, he said, "The Shitting In Bushes Without a Permit Fine."

Donna Langevin

The Middle-aged Man in the Sea
for Tai

The middle-aged man in the sea
swims with dolphins
and sings with whales.
I like this better
than Hemingway's house
hung with moose, water buffalo,
gazelle and eland heads,
eyes staring down
at his bare dinner plates
and bottles of emptiness.

The middle-aged man in the sea
would never shoot himself in the head.
He has too much fun in the waves
as he splashes his wife and tests
the tide at the crack of dawn, then rides
a log like a sea-monster
he dragged out from the beach.

When I tell him I'm afraid to swim
because of the *agua malo*
– that blue bubble with tentacles
like the sorrows that sting me in life –
the middle-aged man in the sea
holds out his hands like two starfish
with five radiant rings
forged from silver and turquoise,
and shouts, "Come swim with me."

Merle Hernández González

Saint Love

It's Now or Never
Don't Ask, Give
You'll Receive more
Help, don't Wait for anything
He gives you a Chance to get better every day
Be Kind, be Generous, be Humble, be Grateful
for all the things life gives you
Don't Think more about yourself,
Consider if the people who live near you are happy
Remember,
The Sun doesn't shine only for you
The moon doesn't lighten your night, because you are
Where your treasure is, your heart will be
Life is not easy, but if you want to change
Shall you try?
It's Now or Never
To Her

Manuel de Jesús Velázquez León

Falling Figs

> *and the stars of the sky fell to the earth*
> *as the fig tree sheds its winter fruit*
> *when shaken by a gale*   Is. 34.4; Rev. 6.12.13

Juan Antonio wakes up with his mouth dry. Without turning over, still facing the stars, he blends his arm under the cot, grabs the plastic bottle and gulps down a long sip. Alcohol warms his body in a wave that flows slowly from within up to his limbs. There is little in the bottle. He thinks of tomorrow with distrust; the ration of alcohol has not arrived.

He always appeases the anguish of the small hours with a drink. Then, he keeps awake looking at the sky. All up there is perfect beauty, infinite abundance. He tries to figure out God's ways in the immutable traces of the constellations and pleads Him. Not as they do in the temple, with songs at the rhythm of tambourines, but in whispers.

"My God!" And he begs for water, for food, for alcohol. When he feels asphyxiated by anguish, he implores the Lord to take him to those infinite seas of light that fill heavens.

This night there is something different in the heights. A shudder that comes from the deepest of the height reaches him. He gazes attentively. He had never seen so many stars as tonight. They extend in clouds of luminous dust everywhere, they bulge the sky downwards with so much weight. Only the almighty power of the Lord can keep the stars from falling like a rain of fire burning and ravaging everything. A muffled thunder comes from the masses of stars. He feels how the cosmic equilibrium that keeps the heavens in their place cracks and splits.

He jumps from the cot. Unable to find the slippers in the dark, he hurries, barefooted and naked towards the house. He pushes the door but Eusebia has put the crossbar so that he cannot enter. "Open the door, Eusebia!" He shouts, "Open it!" Nobody answers from the house in darkness.

Early next day, Eusebia sends him to the store with a bottle for the ration of oil. Nightly fears water down in daily light. The neighborhood is the same old thing: the unpaved streets, the shacks in never-ending construction, the lazy guys dressed in short pants sitting on the street doors. In the newsstand, the line of grimy, unshaven old men waiting for the newspaper to buy it at twenty cents and resell it at one peso each.

It is the last day of the month and there are many people in the store. By then, people scarcely have anything to eat and they are sold their rations a day before scheduled. They brought rice, beans and brown sugar. Juan Antonio has no bags for those things. Besides, Eusebia gave him the exact amount of money for the oil so that he could not buy alcohol in the black market. He has to make the line anyway. In the store, the same neighbors: the toothless old women; the scruffy, smelly people, with their dirt-colored faces because of smoking and poorly eating. Everything as usual.

They talk: the truck that brings water is not coming; there is a brawl in the kerosene line; today the neighborhood has its scheduled blackout; they stole Felo's pig "Even though they penned it in the kitchen at night!" They say that the government will give an extra pound of rice per person until August. An unkempt old man with a grimy straw hat says that it rained burning sand in Potrerillo last night; there were dead birds in the fields this morning. No news about the alcohol; they say that the ration is delayed because they closed the sugar mills.

In the afternoon, he visits Domingo to see what he can get. His pal lives under the Twelve Story Building, in front of the hospital. The building rests upon two-meters-tall pillars. In the space between the floor and the first floor, some friends sleep in beds of rags and jute sacs. Long ago, they drank their properties, their families, their friends, their trust. They pick food leftovers in the trash bins or visit someone who still helps them. Whatever they find to eat or drink, the cigarette butts they pick in the street, they share all in a cooperative. Eusebia hates Domingo. She says that Juan Antonio will end like him; he will sell everything to buy rum and will go to live in the street.

Juan Antonio talks with his pals for a while. He accepts a couple of drinks of "lousy". Lousy is a watery, insipid drink that turns his stomach and fosters his want for a real drink. It is prepared with the medicine for lice they sell in the pharmacy that contains fine alcohol plus the staining sap of the plantain tree. They say that lousy is better than the alcohol they sell to kindle the kerosene stove, which has kerosene so that people do not drink it. You may filter it through sour milk or charcoal and it will still have some kerosene. Domingo says that Juan Antonio has his body covered with reddish swellings because of that stove alcohol. The fact is that you can get it cheap. When they bring the ration, you can buy a bottle for five pesos only. When you get used to it, it does not taste that bad any more.

Eusebia lets him sleep with her when he is sober, but that night Juan Antonio goes again to the cot in the yard. The vast stellar ocean has descended dangerously, but he does not feel any sign of imminence. He spends the night in intermittent dreams, in despair for a drink, without relief.

That Saturday he works as an assistant to the Old Man. The Old Man has been like a father to him. From him Juan Antonio learned masonry, carpentry. Whenever the Old Man finds a good job, he gives Juan Antonio participation. Besides, he helps Eusebia with food. By the end of the month, when the situation is desperate, he always comes to Juan Antonio's house with a bag full of victuals from the little farm that he has near town. He never charges anything for the things that he brings.

They work plating the table of a kitchen. By mid-morning, they take a break, seat among the bits of glazed tiles to have a snack with what they brought. Juan Antonio talks of his fears. He can only tell Old Man about that. The man listens to him in silence while he chews his bread. He has never heard of falling stars. Nevertheless, in Cortadera, where he has relatives, things have fallen from the sky. The day before, the fields were covered by black dust. In the afternoon, stones in flames fell, some peasant hovels were set on fire. He heard that all that comes from a volcano's eruption. "What is a volcano?" Juan Antonio does not know either.

He gets home with a fever; he has no inclination for food. Eusebia makes some beverage for him, but she knows well whence his discomfort comes from. It is Saturday, he has to bathe, wear long pants and shirt to go to the temple.

There are many dressed, perfumed people there. There are people standing in the alleys, many have to listen to the service from the street. Juan Antonio had never seen the temple like this. It is a hectic service. The Pastor is a small, bald man, with a shrill voice. But his fervor makes him grow, roar. He talks of wars, earthquakes, floods, volcanoes, and the lack of faith. He says that these are signs of the coming millennium. He describes the serpent, the horses of Apocalypses. He announces the last horror, the celestial fire: "Sodom and Gomorra have been reborn! Destroy them, Lord, destroy them!" At the end, the congregation scatters without the usual good-bye groups, as if everyone hurried to a refuge.

Juan Antonio feels worse when he returns from the temple, but he says nothing to Eusebia. He goes with his cot to the yard. He has feverish shivers. With his hand, he looks for the bottle under the cot, by sheer instinct. There is nothing.

The floor shakes. He sits up on the cot but dizziness does not let him stand up. Beyond the municipal rubbish dump that is besides his house, in the distant hill where people who have recently come from the countryside have built shacks, there is a fire. Tiny black figures run among the houses on fire. Dizziness increases, he has to lie down on the cot again, facing the sky. The refulgent groove of a falling star illuminates the fields for a few seconds. The flaming spiral swiftly rushes beyond the horizon and the cot's fabric records the tremor of the floor. The constellations slowly distort in front of his eyes. The commotion of the great stellar clusters increases announcing the coming cataclysm. He closes his eyes.

"My God!" And he begs for the stars to hurl down to earth from all the corners of space, to fill the night with billions of luminous strokes in a burning hailstorm that scorches everything alive.

Yanet Alejo Milian

The Countryside

Drops of water falling
immortal gift from the clouds
sublime Royal Palm
clinging to this ground.

Parched maize field
forgotten by men
green left and right
the heat burns my forehead.

Tears of June
along irrigated crops
birds refuse to celebrate
plucked rooster out of tune.

Dust adheres to feet
dirt roads inviting
abandoned windmill
ten heads of cattle under a tree.

Spring becomes a deep desire
bugs carrying their food
a caterpillar inside its dark world
dragonflies dancing.

Deborah Panko

Northumberland's Highway of Heroes

Under rain-soaked umbrellas
strangers on a bridge
reporters taking pictures

From Trenton to Toronto
black processional
past hay-stack hills, childhood lakes

Where trees give way to six lanes
true patriot love
one future, one uniform

Repatriated soldiers
relayed past hamlets
named Welcome, Precious Corners

Following tours through lamp lit
Arabian nights
fabled flying carpet ride

Yellow ribbon of traffic
Greenbelt's green road signs
web of comfort, compliance

Keith Inman

A Weight of Dignity
after a poem by Wang Fan-Chih

On a side road in Cuba
our plush
air-conditioned bus waits
beside a lean stall sparse
with harsh-skinned vegetables
and a leg of ham hung
out of the sun.

A fender-patched '59
paint-brushed Bel Air sits
at the broken curb
where weeds have spilled down
webbing the concrete.

A belly-bent horse pulling itself
to a stop at the stand, huffs
and puffs, its eyes bulging.
It seems amazed to be alive.
The hard, thin trader and young
seller throw their hands toward a deal,
sheet of tin for food.

A few snaps of the reins and the car
axle-d, horse-drawn cart loaded
with prized junk is coaxed away, the horse
remembering muscle remembering
a front left wheel, tread bare
from a jarred bearing restarting
its wobble up the avenue.

I think of the indignity
of the horse forced
to carry this human refuse, but there
across the market square

a pile of sticks rides on a man.

Miriam E. Vera Delgado

Across the Rainbow
To Herbert...until then

One day...
We'll all meet again
Across the Rainbow...
"In the fourth unknown
Dimension
Where all the dead birds sing".
There... where all the birds
With their beautiful colors
And different chirpings
Make happy the day...
Where the fantastic
Vegetation shines
In all its shades of green...
Where the flowers bloom
All year long...
We'll all meet again...
One day...
Across the Rainbow.

Paulos Ioannou

The Only Thing

The only thing she had left to sell
to survive in this marketplace was her body.
The one with the almond eyes,
blue like the pristine waters of the ocean,
the lips red as ripe cherries,
the elegantly shaped breasts round
and graceful like an overripe melon.
A flawless slender figure ready
to be touched caressed and   violated
under the sun's rays or the shadows of the moon.

This is the price of civilization
this the price of enforced austerity
this is the price of fiscal forces.

Thankfully for now
in the prime of her youth
she had a plethora of
competitive advantages
in this marketplace and she
could compete with anybody on body charms.

Roger Langen

Beothuck luck

the Germans couldn't do it to the Jews
although their policy was robust
the Hutu couldn't do it to the Tutsi
although they hacked and hacked
the Khmer Rouge couldn't kill their own
nor the Americans the hamlets of the Viet Cong
the Spanish failed in Peru

everywhere Stalin's ice pick turns to rust
the songs of slaughter sung by Genghis Khan
exhaust, are out of tune
the melody of women and children
whose deaths make history's glory
dissonant, unheard

let's face it

whether for sport or thought or Lebensraum
in whatever hues of ethnic excuse
whether by pliers or firing squad, soft-lettered laws
or tanks or camps, white phosphorous rain
the extermination of a subject people
is difficult to do

still in St. John's, Newfoundland
the sketch artist, Shanawdithit, talented
died in 1829
last of her hunted kind
leaving but a likeness of her mother
60 years on from the Nakba
the promise of another
apogee, Beothuck luck
in Palestine, the dream of another people
cleansed from the land

Tara Kainer

The Welcoming Committee

Here they are to welcome
me back for another
summer at the edge
of the water waving
excitedly in the wind
chattering
in escalating crescendos
my old familiar friends
these trees – balsam poplars,
yellow birch, trembling aspens.
In the distance movement
across the lake
above the variegated
evergreens, nine stacked &
circling, like jets coming in
for a landing, large, even
from here. A hawkish summer.

Prompted by my cottage
reading
I name them: Hamid (Karzai),
Charles (Koch), Silvio (Berlusconi),
Angela (Merkel), Kim (Jong-Un),
Vladimir (Putin), David (Cameron),
Benjamin (Netanyahu), Stephen
(Harper). I swim closer
get a better look
at the opposite shore.

No. Not hawks.

Vultures.

Raymond Fenech

This will never happen to me syndrome

The taste of death won't go away. There is Christmas, Easter and Valentine but also depressing advertisements about cancer. Outside - the slime and sleet - endless winter. Never before had I seen all this from the current perspective. Yet, I'm weighted down moving forward, backwards, dropping on my knees struggling to my feet, to stay up, only to be knocked down again. It all started when I began losing weight. I tried to emulate my hero Rocky Balboa, his joy of living, winning against all odds. But how can one train to fight cancer? I screamed in a baritone voice hoping my serenade would turn into a grenade, wake up the people who worry about trivialities make them realize that health is never a sacrosanct right. But they all suffer from the, "this will never happen to me syndrome!" Hodgkin's Lymphoma and a stroke broke me down into shards, like a fallen porcelain moon. And I thought I was high and dry on my way to a new red summer dawn - could already feel the warmth. I was derailed, impaled by the sword of fate. Now, I stand again, shrug off the pain trying to regain, to cease, to feign, change a sorrowful sunset, into a happy refrain. My heart sinks at this every passing day, be it summer, the fall, winter or spring. Each time there is a freeze, snow knee deep, I grit my teeth, uplift my frightened heart and try to smoulder its weakened beat.

The day dawns with difficulty to breathe, freezing cold, incontrollable shakes and profuse sweating, the long endless rest on a hospital bed. There are plastic flowers in the vase, which I envy for their immortality - the stench of surgical spirit. Fourteen hours of painful chemotherapy: dripping orange liquid and a torturous injection that lasts five minutes. I am forced to listen to my heart beat, stare at the blood stain on the carpet from my punctured arm whilst trying to find a non-thrombosed vein ... Should I immerse myself into a sob story no one wants to hear, start over standing tall, even if I fall, or wait for another dawn? Time has clipped Pegasus's wings, his unicorn trimmed. So I will call out my fearsome 300 Spartans to turn this scuffle into a last spectacular tussle.

K. V. Skene

Where Sea Ends

We go down to the sea
to feel it flow
in and through and out
and back into blue.

> *Where sea ends*
> *and sky begins*
> *unravels at twilight.*

And you are barely there
against me and you breathe
the sweat-soft air, surrender
to sea.

> *Where shore ends*
> *and sea begins*
> *unwinds in moonlight.*

If you leave, when
you leave, I will have to remember
how I lived before
I had you.

> *Where you end*
> *and I begin –*
> *undone by midnight.*

More and more I learn the lie,
the words tasted, swallowed
unspoken, the smell of sorrow
on skin ...

> *Where love ends*
> *hate begins*
> *unfolding the dawn.*

Heide Brown

Synchronicity in Cuba

A quiet Canadian
        I sit and write
                in welcome shade
        sheltered from loud tourists
                by fluttering palms and
                a variety of tropical species
        unknown to me.

        I dream
                of sharing my memories
        more specifically
        my Cuban memories.

        I dream
                of finding a publisher
                who would be enthusiastic about
        printing my writings
                        in Canada and also
                        in Cuba.

Enraptured in my dream
        I become aware
                of a group at the next table
                        also writing.

A writer's group perhaps
and they sound Canadian . . .

Swallowing my shyness
I introduce myself and, from this point on
synchronicity unfolds.

I find,
    not just any Writer's Group
        a Canadian Writer's Group
            with the Canada Cuba Literary Association.

I find friends.

I find publishers
        in Canada, and
        in Cuba.

Synchronicity
        has manifested
            my dreams.

Kimberley Grove

A look at country living in Canada

I sat at the kitchen table, the heart of the home, looking at black and white snapshots of the old community, churches, barns and buildings that are no more. Bill Finley regaled the story of his valiant attempt to save the old big white Baptist Church up the street. He drove down with as many fire extinguishers as he could manage. "Almost put her out," he said, "but I ran out of extinguishers. That fire was so hot that it started to melt the tail lights of my car. It's amazing that my car didn't explode."

It was my task to learn something of the past of Northumberland County from some residents who have lived here most of their lives. Bill Finley who was Reeve and mayor of Grafton for 35 years and his sister Joan who was mayor of Cobourg for 6 six years agreed to tell me about my new homeland.

We started with their lives as children in these parts. They would wander through farmers' fields not worrying about being kidnapped or caught for trespassing. They were carefree days that ended with a swim in Shelter Valley Creek in the summertime. "Everyone was poor in those days so we weren't comparing clothes or houses," said Bill.. "We had electricity but a lot of our neighbours didn't. It wasn't uncommon for people not to have indoor plumbing. We'd march up the street like a human train to the old Wicklow Public School – a one room school house. It was a great way to learn because when you were finished your work you could listen in to the lesson of the next grade up. You could pick up as much as you wanted." The walk home was interrupted by stopping in at someone's house for a cookie.

There were often three generations living in one house, so the grandmother living there became known as everyone's grandma. "There was Grandma Wilson and Kernagh and Finley."

Most of the children lived on the farms. Weekends were spent picking apples, feeding the animals, or tending to the crops. "We were more self-sustained in those days." Food was plentiful. Entertainment was local. Every community had their own baseball team. Everything we needed was local. One man made his living making ladders for the apple farms. "Everyone was so resourceful. Every school had their Christmas concerts. Now days if you had something like that you'd have to go to court," said Joan.

The trains were more important in the days past. Dairy farmers would take their milk to the train going to Toronto. There were no quotas in those days so you could sell as much as you milked. "The 1950s were the best days for farmers. There wasn't the competition that there is today. Now it's the big farms that are buying up all the little farms.

Children are driven or travel by school bus. Trains carrying oil or imported products whizz by the towns and hamlets. Canada's farms have exchanged hay for homes, lots of new development for duplicate housing projects or windmill structures. The people of Canada are in danger of becoming food hostages to other nations. There was nostalgia in what they shared and as I picked up my papers to leave I wondered if we have shredded a lot of the good of the past in our present passion for our technological progress.

Katharine Beeman

My neighbours
never play dominoes on Tuesday

Below my Havana window
the dominoes chunk
indistinct voices drift up.
It's Tuesday.
My neighbours never
play dominoes on Tuesday.
Today, Hugo Chávez died.
Like missing a step on the stair
grief shakes us
into a new dimension
where my neighbours
play dominoes on Tuesday.

Manuel Velázquez León

Thank God for Peace

Dear Tai,

It rained today, after a few days of 35ºC afternoon heat, the cool rain reprieve was welcome, though our cave is most often fresh. Last night we cooked tamales and some lean pork in a rich tomato sauce. We also had coffee milk, it goes well with tamales. I know you like my coffee milk. When we have nice food and it rains the universe seems a smaller place, childhood is closer, the farm, Mother cooking wonderful food, as she always did, while it rains in the fields. Father arriving on his horse under the rain in the late afternoon. The world out there is cold or brutally hot, as it is in the Middle East in these days. Here, there is peace, thank God, it is sweet to be home with Adonay and Pablo when it rains. Brother, I saved a couple of tamales for you, just in case.

Brother Manuel.

James Deahl

Unread Books

A novel from childhood — *A High Wind in Jamaica* — a story the man had never read, came to him again on the hundredth anniversary of the Great Storm of 1913. As it had been back then, this was also a night of blind tempest, wind tearing through the upper limbs of leaf-shorn oaks and maples, shearing branches from towering balsam poplars. "A high wind" he said to himself as midnight drew near and the November gale refused to abate. Indeed, it would grow ever stronger as the night wore on. He had been reading "Album Leaf" by Robyn Sarah, a piece on how the storm of Nazism, as if by malign sorcery, changed a charm of good fortune into an emblem of death: a storm of hate that forever transformed Europe, a storm he was conceived within during the snow squalls in early March of the year Hitler died. Odd how events could alter everything, topple the stoutest trees, flatten homes, displace whole populations, and destroy one world so that a new world could arise from the void. Stranger still how a book never read can colour a life.

Today the man lives in a small town far from the city of his birth, in a different country, with a new wife more beautiful than any woman he could have ever imagined. The novel was a romance of friendship and deceit on the high seas, a tale of adventure and betrayal, just the thing certain to claim the imagination of a lonely boy. No one can explain why he had not read it during childhood's long years, or why he does not read it now.

Bruce Kauffman

the languages of history

how this afternoon
describes this morning
        is written
        will be told
in a more ancient language
than
how tomorrow
will describe
today

Patrick Connors

Things I Must Be True To

My mind, my reason, my ideas
My morals, my values, my ideals
My heart, my Love, my soul
My spirit, my vision, my dreams
My Mother, my brother, my sister

                              The Father

            My limited understanding
Of the universal flow
                              and
My role in it

                  Those aspects left
Of my long-haired
Coniferous tree-hugging
Hippie mantra
                        and my
Toronto Maple Leaf loving
                              ingrown
Hockey-haired mullet

                  My family
Genealogical, spiritual, ecumenical
Incidental, philosophical, animal
Commercial, longitudinal, municipal
My neighbourhood, my country, my world
                  And all who are in it

My passions, my reasons, my causes
The issues that I take issue with
That which ensues from that which I issue

I stand up for
The cause and effect
Of that which I stand for

                              Truth

Before I can do this
                    While I aspire to all that
At the end of the day
                              Myself

Yanet Alejo Milian

Morning Picture

I walk through my city
leaving broken walls
humble faces and hands

People going to work
little boy in a red uniform
hidden marbles in his pockets

Delicious fragrance spreads
mixture of our routine,
a wrinkled smile

Neighbors sharing their coffee,
loud sounds everywhere,
dogs barking to strangers

Black and white skin as one blood
drums and guitars
drowned hopes inside

Tracks of pain in grey eyes
unknown future to some,
sad expressions behind bars

Glasses of rum waiting
cheap tobacco giving pleasure
a careless mustache

Promises brighten in candles
prayers to African orishas
necklaces in all colours

Hearts yearning in the distance,
eternal lines around
pictures of Che on T-shirts

Perfect symphony of daily life
I see the streets and cars
solitary arms

A faded Cuban flag in front,
spiritual scene in our veins,
children playing under the rain

Patrick Connors

Somewhere Down the Zen River

Current runs smoothly
all stands still for a moment—
the eternal now

June Salmon

Morning Rising

With new dawn reluctant waking
these last few days of summer,
mysterious silver gauze conceals island shapes
not far from shore but hidden now
as if they never were
or had been last night
before the curtain fell, bringing
an impossible sky
so full of starry light
it took breath away.
Now uniform grey belies
earthly beauty I behold day after day
through my all-season watch
when crystal is the catchword:
crystal clarity of snowcap
crisp-fresh, dew-glistened green of spring
blood-rust sheen of decay shining through fall's chill.
Nothing can match end of summer sun
burning off morning mist,
slowly lifting,
revealing nature's perfect soul:
morning rising.

Brian Gordon Sinclair

Hemingway's Hot Havana

Shark Attack

House lights out. Stage lights on. Hemingway enters stage left. As he takes a drink from the stage right table, the music fades. He approaches the audience.

Well, I produced three sons. How did you make out?

(He puts the drink down and steps forward.)

Most of all, I enjoyed the summers. That's when my sons came fishing with me, all three of them. Jack...who did not want to be called Bumby anymore, Patrick or Mouse, whose very difficult birth gave me the ending for my novel, *A Farewell to Arms*, and Gregory, my youngest boy, or Gig as we called him.

Gig was born to be wicked but I loved him. He was my son and I loved him...and I will never forget the time that I had to prove that love.

On this particular trip, the morning fishing had been lousy, so after lunch, we all decided to go spearfishing, right on the edge of the Gulf Stream and none of that modern stuff with air tanks...just goggles and good, old fashioned, homemade spears. Mostly we speared yellow tails and snappers and grunts. Grunts are those funny little ones. When you take them out of the water, they make an almost human sound, bit like a belch.

(He belches.)

Most of the fish were harmless and swam in big schools, thousands of them but sometimes a barracuda would get closer than you wanted. The main danger from cudas came when you entered the water too suddenly. They'd snap at you and run off but not before stopping and turning to look at you, with a piece of your thigh in their mouth.

By this time, Gregorio Fuentes was my first mate. He'd take the dinghy part way out from *The Pilar* and pull the fish off the boy's spears. The two older boys were tall enough to touch the reef bottom but Gig was only four and a half feet tall. He had to expend a lot of energy just keeping himself afloat. That's when he came up with what he thought was this very clever idea for storing the fish. He unbuckled his belt, put the end through the fish's mouth, pulled it out through the gill, and then re-buckled it. That way, he could store three or four fish before he had to make the fifty yard swim back to the dinghy.

After spearing four grunts, he suddenly noticed that there wasn't another fish in sight. How could that many fish disappear that fast? Then he saw why. Three huge sharks, each more than eighteen feet long were coming toward him in a slow S-shaped curve. The scent of the fish blood was calling them.

Gig screamed, uncontrollably, again and again, more terrified than he'd ever been in his whole life. Even over the sound of the waves, I heard him. "What is it, Gig"?

"Sharks, sharks," he cried, "three big ones."

"Okay, pal, take it easy," I said. "Throw something at them to get their attention and swim to me". He pulled the grunts off his belt and tossed them toward the sharks. Now, Gig wasn't much of a swimmer but this time he set a new record in getting to me. I hoisted him up on my shoulders which were barely out of the water with his weight and started thrashing towards the dinghy. It was my body that was under the surface. The sharks would get me first, not Gig. Sure I was scared, but I had to save him. Gig snuck a look back over his shoulder and saw the sharks devour the grunts. Then they turned and started toward us again. Finally, I made it to the edge of the dinghy. Gregorio pulled Gig in and then they both hauled me aboard…just at the exact moment when the first shark slapped up against the side of the boat.

(He claps his hands.)

Phew!

Later, when Gig told me about the dead fish on his belt, I gave him one hell of a bawling out. But it didn't matter. My boy was alive and he knew that I cared.

I don't know what I'd do if I lost one of my sons.

Do you?

Paul R. Carr

Life

Knocking at heaven's door

R a i s e s   t h e   q u e s t i o n

of   hell

and life
and time
and truth
and reason
and hatred
and purpose
and   why?
and   whose God?
and   whose heaven?
and   whose what?

To live for life
waiting for afterward
can be
another way
of not living

                        life.

Brian Mullally

Sounds Astray

When I wake in the night to the screech of a train
The noise has me baffled as it pours in my brain
Until I remember, I'm lying in bed
And it isn't a trumpet call from the dead
Hear it clatter and chatter and pass on its way
Leaving me wondering where sounds go astray
Where does sound go when it leaves my ear?
High in the sky in the atmosphere?
Where are the sounds of my boyhood mode?
The ring of steel horseshoes along the road
The clang of the blacksmith's hammer; the hiss of steam
They are long gone and departed like last night's dream
The chuckle of a spring, bubbling free
Squelch of mud when it's up to your knee
The whir of a wing when the bird is disturbed
The call of the woodpigeon is seldom heard
The echoing birdsong when it greets the dawn
The chirp of a cricket on a summer lawn
The rustle of leaves before they fall
That crackling wood fire out in the hall
Coyotes crying out in the wild
A crooning woman nursing her child
My mother humming a gypsy strain
My father's sad song in a tipsy vein
Listen how I whistle on the way to school
Can you feel the breeze of an evening cool?
Did you hear the splash of fish on a hot summer's day?
Hear the lingering lament of the loon far away
Where does sound go when it leaves this place?
A celestial market in outer space?
Should I climb to the stars and stack up my cart?
Or lay on my back and fill up my heart

K. V. Skene

Miles

of white-powder sand,
a blue on blue horizon
and the long-forgiving roll
of a southern sea. Shadows stalk
our half-forgotten footprints
heading nowhere
up the beach
and down and the nightwind
silkens our arms and shoulders
as the bloody sun
drops
suddenly
out of sight – our hands reach,
find, hold each other
in the dark. Tonight
it's easy
to be happy, easy
to remember love.

Deborah Panko

Meditation
on the 'Occupy' Movement

Seeds scatter, rain falls.
A tree grows from root to leaf
gives breath of life
feet to fingertips alight
time, space occupied
saints and parasites alike.

Flesh bound and air bent
fruit of earth's womb, we are rags
and bones on wooden ladders.
'Ascend' say the soothsayers
your towers of fear
palisade of pointed spears.

Call it divine right:
bodies risen
bodies incorporated
a wall of streets trading
magic words, law's wizardry
ramparts of paper

skyscrapers climbing
ticker tape doling dollars
– spun by who eats well
judging who will eat at all –
frantic, loud, breathless
pavement strewn with adbusters.

Tell us what you want
what to remember
of leaf, tree, sun overhead
of soup bowls, burn-barrels.

Hugh Hazelton

Horror Vacui

— inspired by the poet Louise Haley (Meow)
—"At least I was being paid to be a zombie!"
Doug Winspear, commenting on the trip home
after working all day as a film extra

The vampires forever plot to find
new sources of blood
the blood of others, of course, fresh and red,
pumping from ingenuous veins.
They've convened V-8s, V-20s and IVF summits
in mountain castle hideaways, desert towers of glass
and monster city hotels where they
quibble and nibble clotted canapés among the
leeches and sip vintage *cépage*, wiping the bubbling
hemoglobin from their lips with fine linen.
They wax sanguine conversing
on blood lines and bloodpower
as they straighten the knots of their blood ties
and dig into their blood pudding
discussing plasma screen presentations
on trickle-down theory
controlled gushers frackline extraction dual-flow
pipelines and giant blood vessel terminals
as the crowds wail and lament in the streets below
protesting the how many hundred thousand billion
barrels flowing from their factories that squeeze
every drop and corpuscle from pallid labourers
working frantically alongside implacable robots
and then pour the viscous ooze into underground
vaults, the gold standard of blood diamonds
dug from the deepest veins and liquefied for
transport to industrial heartlands.
"It's never really enough," they say, as they lay in
supplies for a thousand ten thousand a million years,
"You've got to pump out every drop for possible

panic buying insecurity emergencies."
Stock up stock markets stock yards be ready for the
future of the genetically fortunate few who ride
glistening on fossil fluids along major arteries.
"Oil is in my blood," they nod over Bloody Caesars,
"and it's almost as good" —
boiling the soil, injecting chemicals into aquifers,
blowing up shale, perforating the sea
all to siphon off the muck of ancient oceans jungles
dead Triassic bodies into their thirsting engines.
"Those rebellions in the empty lands make my blood
boil: the primitives just don't know what's good for
them — Send in the Werewolf Weremacht with the
killing machines and rip the opposers to shreds,
get their warblood up on hypersteroids and
psychodrugs, preach to them with hatefeel
and set them loose on the countryside
with nighttime vision and robot wings to hunt the
outliers down, licensed to killmaimtorturerape
ordered to do whatever it takes because
WE MUST HAVE BLOOD!
now and always."
And near dawn, when it's late, the hemodelegates go
off to bed in their five-drop cavernous hotel rooms
humming the theme song to "Mask of the Red
Death" and lie cuddled up munching the red-filled
chocolates on their pillows
to boost their blood sugar
for blood relations
and relax watching zombie movies:
"I love those proliferations of the living dead
with my apologies of course to the poor *houngan*
who told me it's a perversion of true *vodûn*.
That's so, I replied, but the hoarding of lifeblood and
essential oils is a perversion too,

though one the world needs in order to generate
the thirst for power
just as cashflow and liquid assets and bloody-
mindedness keep finances flowing,
so let's watch the zombie crowds getting dispatched
at will —who cares? They're all dead anyway,
though not of course in the way we are:
a marvelous metaphor for the way it actually works.
What a goof on the proles:
Better kill as many as you can before they get you!
One bite is mortal and the mindless things just keep
on coming like starving people hungry for work
or bloodless bodies bereft of liquid gold —
Ah, but I've got a Power Point to give tomorrow
on the effect of heartlessness on blood flow,
and it's time to whisper the vampire vow
that no one will ever find out what we really do
or who we really are —
it's a secret we take with us to the grave
for future undead generations,
so come now let us sleep
and sleep and sleep
slipping again forever into
the eternal unconscious."

George Arnold

Fair Southern Flower

Fair southern flower I see you bloom
Your countenance lights up my day
And with your smile defeats the gloom
Of troubles met along the way

Your eyes burn bright with blush of youth
And sometimes fade to limpid pools
To steal my heart and then forsooth
To twinkle like a sparkling jewel

Your ginger curls they frame your face
And emphasize your calming power
You are a gift from heaven's grace
His gift to me, fair southern flower

Raymond Fenech

Mama's Last *Appassionata*
to my mother

Beethoven's Appassionata reverberated
sweeping from wall to wall,
as I stood silent in the hall,
thinking she'll never play this tune anymore.

Music scores opened where she'd last played
with gusto, love and pain
when her arthritic fingers
touched down heavily on every note,
like an uncontrollable weight.

Recalled how her frail figure would emerge
smiling into the sun filled hall,
as I knocked gently on the glass door,
almost afraid of smoldering the tune,
now realizing this scene was a *déjà vu*.

Outside, a cacophony of sounds
far from *Beethoven*, *Mozart* or *Bach*,
a pollution of noise drowned the past,
all that was noble of value that lasts.

Those early summer mornings
when *Ix-Xejka** limped up the porch
fresh *sargu** in hand; his dog waited on the stairs,
as he wrapped the fish in newspaper,
then hobbled away to our next door neighbour.

The house had stood strong through decades and more
its walls like a fortress now thick with moss;
crevices now empty of crickets that chirped,
each time the summer night crept gently from light
while mama's fingers played us a lullaby.

Beethoven's Appassionata reverberated
through these double built walls,
my refuge for decades from spring to the fall;
now this last melody as the curtains are drawn.

*

*Ix-Xejka was the nickname of an old fisherman, Karmnu (Charles) who
lived in a very small room with his small black dog close to my house.*

Sargu (Sunbream) – a very fine fish very popular in Maltese cuisine.

Paulos Ioannou

In Every Corner There Is a Woman

In every corner there is a woman
yesterday, today and tomorrow

there is always a woman
standing at the corner
breastfeeding the newborn
the pain and the pleasure

there is a girl holding
the hem of her dress
tomorrow she would be standing at the corner
breastfeeding a newborn

the man is absent
he is the emptiness
in these streets of melancholy and despair
he has a window to look outside
as all men wont to do

will he open the door
will he invite her in
or will he call the police to
remove the nuisance

Heide Brown

Cuban Beach in February

Winter wind whips
thick clouds
across the sky.

Ocean's appetite is aroused.
Hungry tongues
clutch and suck
pulling me towards
her waiting white arms.

Wency Rosales

The Soft Veil of the Rainbow

Walking slowly down the white foaming seashore,
I feel the water wipes away the traces
of your naked soul.
Far behind slips my silhouette trying to fit
into what is left from your sacred past,
trying to fit into what is left with no choices.
The seagull catches the given gift
in the surface of the sea
while the soft dance the ocean's rhythms, the chorus
of the corals raise the tune of a crescendo ,
DO RE MI FA SOL.
In an organic symphony that whistles
the forbidden legend of our ancestors.
The drums beat announcing you are leaving.
The crimson horizon weeps salty tears
while the sadness covers my pain like if it were
the soft veil of the rainbow.

Donna Langevin

Car Cuba

cars crusted with sea-salt
guano and sand
Ladas on their last tires
30's and 40's Dodges
finned and flaking Buicks
Chevies with grinning grills

cars that run on willpower
wired like your worst nerves
cars that trust to luck
and cars with too much Attitude
that tailgate the wind

cars that have no seatbelts
cars with bad-ass brakes
that paint the highways red
or poison you with fumes
leaking through floors

cars humming tunes without radios
cars that fold like accordions

cars as brave as the people
who survive cold war
independent cars
with nine lives of their own

cars with missing headlights
exhaust pipes, mirrors, fenders
bumpers and bald tires
cars that wait for transplants

cars that believe in miracles
and rise from the dead
cars held together
with cardboard, coat hangers, duct tape
and string filched from kites
that soar over the waves lapping at Havana
as you fly down the Malecón
stomach in your throat

Keith Inman

The Banes Bullfinch
Bullfinch's try to out-sing their rivals

Outside Fidel's church
a house has become a restaurant,
best paint in town. We talk
about schooling, health,
economy without corruption.
A bird in a cage high up
on the wall begins to sing.

We order food and discuss
the difference of ration dis-
tributed through duty
and social programs dia-framed
through taxes. The bird in the cage
high up on the wall sings louder.

A story of revolution is told.
no sentries posted, the flight
of the marshes, small
groups under stray bullets
shredding the cane, until
they made the mountain, counted
themselves alive. High up
in the woven cage against a bright
blue wall the song of a little
brown bird demands to be heard.

We drink Cerveza's and share
plantain, our repast served.

Miriam E. Vera Delgado

Emptiness

I feel so weak…
I'm full of emptiness…
Desperately I pray for:
A drop of Joy
A mirage of Love
A sprinkle of Star Dust
A spell of Crazy Happiness
A gust of Passion
A Ray of Sun
A Shooting Star
A dream of Fantasy
If they come and fill me…
Then I can climb mountains!

Merle Hernández González

The Stony Heart

Today I realize you'll never change
It's a sad reality for all
It's a sad reality for me
That I thought you'd break the chrysalis
To exhibit your beautiful wings
How is it possible you always strike
The hearts that love you with no measure,
The hands that want to help you
Without asking any thing
Only a lily mind like mine
Could think your actions would be better.
It's time to take the stony heart out of your flesh,
And change it for a purely human heart.

Raúl Vera Delgado

Love Formula

The architecture of perfect love
Is a well-known recipe.
Knowing that violence,
death and suffering
Only engender new and bigger failures
The adequate formula was created
With a compound of wonderful elements:
Absorbing during 33 years enough pain,
happiness, sweetness, admiration and reasoning;
Hang from a wooden cross amidst the deepest suffering,
Resurge and spread in the Universe as a celestial offering;
Emanating love and confidence in big amounts in all directions...
And Forgive.

James Deahl

Vermont Slate

Four shards of slate taken from a site on the Vermont shore of Lake Champlain within sight of Quebec now lie on a backyard table in Sarnia, near the shore of Lake Huron some sixty miles north of Detroit. The slate was formed under conditions of unimaginable pressure and heat long before people existed. For unknown years it endured the harsh reality of winter gales driven down from Canada.

Today the shards endure the heat of a Midwest summer. The edges appear sharp as surgical instruments but are rather dull. Slate will not hold an edge as well as flint. Unitarians love slate because it cannot be used as a tool to skin an animal; ideal for roofs, it has no military applications. Inside the rock are tiny crystals too small to see. Within these microscopic rooms, the life of the spirit continues. Gas and dust clouds collapse, swirling ever faster; tides of energy wash in and out like the vast tides at Fundy.

Sliced and polished, slate formed the blackboards of my youth. In the deserted classrooms of late afternoon, chalk dust finally settling, I could begin to catch the spirit singing.

Roger Langen

Samson's hair

the hero's curse
to leave blood on the hands
a weight upon the soul
of remembered wrongs

in a quiet house in Gaza
a harlot plays with Samson's hair
who knows what they say to each other
with what coarseness or comfort the evening passes
she is invisible, Philistine, he a biblical superman
contemplating his terrible destiny
to be human somehow and a judge
a strong man bringing doom

tent or temple both must fall
in Israel's hand
the heart that keeps on beating
is Palestine's

Brian Gordon Sinclair

Easter Rising:
The Last Words of Patrick Pearse (Act II)
Exerpt

"When evening arrived, the gunfire seemed to slacken. (Gentle) As I looked round at the men and women, I became convinced that they would all perish in this Rising and I had brought them here. Now I make no attempt to deny responsibility for the death and destruction of the Rising. The only question is this: How will it appear in the eyes of God? We are after all, waging a war, and the church has never forbidden war so long as it is fought for a worthy cause. Can anyone doubt that the freedom of Ireland is a worthy cause? We are fighting for our lives and we are willing to die, if need be, as a sacrifice to that cause.

We are willing to die as thousands before us have died. When Cromwell came to Ireland his aim was the complete extermination of the Irish people. His Puritan ministers charged the English army to, and I quote, "To kill all that were, young man and old, children and maiden". They swept across Ireland like the plague.

We are willing to die as millions did during the famine years of Queen Victoria. During her reign alone, one and a quarter million people starved to death when the potato crops failed. Entire families died in the fields with their mouth green from eating grass. Sometimes a child survived, but it is said, not totally in jest, that you can count all the orphans who survived the great hunger, on one set of fingers and toes, and still have three fingers and a toe left over. Three and a half million were evicted from houses they or their fathers had built. All in all, over four million people were forced to flee the country they loved.

More and more, I realised that Ireland could rely only on force, in some form or another, because everything else had failed. Irishmen were simply struggling to keep alive and England deemed it a crime. Surely the people of Ireland deserve redemption after centuries of bondage. If some of us must die to achieve this redemption, so be it. Our purpose is to restore life to Ireland and if the resurrection of Ireland results from the Rising, from the sacrifice of our lives, we will have succeeded.

Bruce Kauffman

languages

dead winter
in a large open room
a fireplace sits
      empty
      cold

a heart
in another room
      the same

what is the language
      of fire

what replaces
its muted words

like a match
is there a single consonant
a single vowel
a single word
      that ignites
      and

what was
that first language

      before fire

Katharine Beeman

El Malecón, Havana

Such is our love

spuming   without horizon

perpetual

amazement

10th Anniversary

One of the special features of being a member in the CCLA is the privilege of travelling as a delegation of Canadian authors and being invited to read at different casual or official functions. The CCLA trip of 2014 was our CCLA 10th Anniversary and hence a very special year. We spent our two weeks in two locations. One week at an all-inclusive beach resort at Guardalavaca and a second week at a small intimate pool side resort called, Villa Mirador de Mayabe, near the small town of Mayabe, 8 km from the city of Holguin, hosted by our dear friend Wency.

During each of the two weeks we had plenty of ocean and pool side relaxing time but we also did readings, workshops and daytrips to see parts of Cuba that a non-delegation tourist might not normally see. We visited Cuban friends in their homes for dinners, coffee and readings, we took private bus excursions to distant locales, we were guided to special out of the way Cubano restaurants where we ate very well indeed.

One request that I made to Bruce Kauffman, the editor of this collection, was that we include a selection of work that was written during, or inspired by, travelling with that CCLA delegation on the 10th Anniversary CCLA trip in 2014. Bruce embraced the idea and has included those inspired works here. Thank you Bruce for being the editor of this special section. We hope you enjoy the following section.

Prez Tai / Richard M. Grove

Richard M. Grove

A Letter Home

Dear Father: Kim and I are in a fancy air conditioned bus driving through the breadbasket of Cuba, the agricultural area in the middle of the island, on our way to Universidad Ciego de Avila. From time to time we drive past a small windmill whirling in the morning breeze. I think you know the kind I mean. The kind we had at the back of our house when we lived on the farm. I remember seeing it from the bathroom window when I was just a boy. As we pass by they are all graciously spinning in the sunrise-gentle wind pumping water for the farms they service. I was trying to remember if the windmill that we had in the backyard actually worked or if it was just a relic of the past, a museum piece, long ago replaced by the electric pump. Somehow I don't ever remember seeing it in motion.

Yesterday Kim and I were introduced to our dormitory room at Universidad Ciego de Avila. The room was optimistically cool. The air conditioner purred quietly to the long blinking florescent bulb that revealed our three-bed room. We were greeted by a modern TV of more than adequate size and a refrigerator of similar dimensions. The definition of an optimist is Kim seeing the TV and totally expecting it to work. The definition of a super optimist is Kim thinking that if you wait a while longer it will warm up and flicker to life. The definition of an uber-super optimist is after the TV has finally turned on that Kim adjusts the rabbit ears expecting to tune in a channel, any channel. The definition of a happy optimist is Kim watching a clear, in focus, Cuban documentary.

The definition of a realist is Kim not expecting water to ever arrive at the air-hissing pipe that dribbles into the bathroom sink.

Your number-one-son, Ricardo.

John B. Lee

Writing the Darkness

I am
there beneath the black scrimshaw
of an overpainting where
the colour comes
at the brilliant reveal
bleeding through
the interstices of a blue scar
the brave
lightline of a luminous
vermillion or one
photosynthetic green vein
like the bent rib
of a living leaf's vivid lightning
this is I
the child amanuensis
of a compass point
in that secretarial knife slice
in that anthracitic scratch
of an unemprisoned hue
the millioning of night
as at one cold moon
a dog's eye weeps
and is blinded by time
old in the bones
like the wind limp
of a broken-branch orchard
the deracinate and desiccated arm
where the sapless
and thereby orphaned
ripening goes on
and is unattended
even as by the glorious rounding out
one sun-pure impregnation of seed-fat
mango glory hangs waiting

to be plucked
and succulent with rot
and a glutinous over-softening

this Cuban dog, the one we call Winky
scrofulous and lousy
flea-swollen
crimson and patchy
with relentless itch
curls down into unborn memory
seeking the sweet respite of sleep
that comes
only to the amniotic
startlement of a first spark
a sperm-pierced ovum
zygotic and then as with
the feral whelp
and a nascent milkening
hunger comes
in lactatory star-swirl to
this love-starved galaxy
where there is already suffering enough
for all

and my octogenarian mother
her mind
oversweetened by loss
dims down to one
sentence
"I am glad to be alive"

and a man I have known
imprisoned by a body
broken at birth
gives hope
the gift of his big attention
and makes me ashamed

no amount
of sinful expiation
in the world of woe
can stop

this jubilant pathos
of lice and tics or make him
refuse
the joyful urgency of tail-whipped appreciation
for meat scrap and
stale white inedible bread
folded over once
like the wincing of the field
what a winnowing
we will do
when with the ineluctable idiocy
of a single death
we fail
the sparrows
and do not hear their song
sewing the winter
with the warp and woof of insouciant white
and the interweaving
of a withering spring

Shane Joseph

The Thin White Line

The man with the machete stares across the thin white line on the road as we travel in opposite directions, me going uphill and him going down. Behind, the cow, with ribs protruding and udders collapsing, follows her master along the path of the only life she has known until she winds up featured on the menu of a restaurant reserved for those who are more equal than others.

The man with the machete locks stares with me and I see the failed promise of 55 years in his eyes, and the fleeting thought that neither of us wants to voice. The wallet full of cash and the passport to a cold but prosperous country protrude from my pocket, announcing their presence loudly. A swing and a hit on this lonely road and he could be onto a home run, out of the ballpark, and my carcass would be left in some secret place to feed the hungry animals of the land. Equalization in one fell swoop: a goal that generations of central planners and millions of bureaucrats have never been able to achieve.

The man with the machete passes me, and the thin white line on the road is our reminder that there is another line, one between barbarism and humanity, and that we are both clinging to the side of the latter, if but for our sanity. Receding footsteps confirm that we are each continuing our journeys, me going uphill and him going down. But I wonder how much hunger the belly can endure before the heart shuts off, the brain freezes and the hand swings viciously. I wonder how long it would be before the man with the machete turns around and crosses that thin white line.

Cynthia Mitchell

Releasing the Dandelion

¡Bienvenido al primer día entero en Cuba! Y el primer día del senti-miento de vida trabajó harmonías. Estoy sentado sobre arena muy suave y blanca. Las olas del océano suena y tengo dos cafés con leche.

Welcome to the first entire day in Cuba! And the first day of feeling life-work harmony. I am sitting on the soft white sand. Listening to the waves of the ocean with two Spanish coffees with milk!

I find myself sitting here in awe of the fact I am sitting here, that I am still risking this journey of following my bliss. That I am into the second semester off from teaching and am now really diving into debt. And where do I find myself? Cuba. Club Amigo Atlantico. One week here and then one week closer to Holguín.

In August I decided to commit to this trip. I am so grateful that I did. I really need to be here. To be inspired to passionately pursue my bliss and let my financial worries go. To really feel what I mean when I say: "Release the Inner Dandelion." Who knows where those seeds will land when they get taken by the wind. Who knows?

But how does it feel? Incredibly freeing as the wind off the ocean blows my hair out of my face and the pages over the pen. As I practice emptying my mind of everything, especially self-doubt. As I unlearn everything, especially what I was schooled to believe. As I listen to people young and old tell me: "Your story must be written." It is true that compassionate people need to find a voice. We need to get control over our Inner Critic and Inner Bully. As for the Inner Dandelion – Yes!!

Let it blossom. Let it fly. The beautiful thing is it can root in the worst conditions – the places where nothing else will grow. The places where your Inner Critic and Bully don't want it to grow. That is the true beauty of the dandelion. Even if you have an Inner Jailer or Inner Abuser, your Inner Dandelion can still take root. Can still seed. Can still get caught up in their hot air and take root again!!

That is the power of your Inner Dandelion, your Inner Passion. It doesn't stop because someone says it is not worthy. It doesn't stop if someone uproots it. It digs in and grows again. Seeds again. Your Inner Dandelion is seeding inside you like crazy. Building up and wanting to explode. Wanting you to give it permission to turn the fields of waste in your mind to fields of beauty in your heart.

The beautiful experience I am having as I feel my Inner Dandelion itself release is the power of possibility – there are so many possibilities!!! And as I learn to stay away from the "what if" thoughts, as I learn to let the seeds of my ideas get caught up in the wind; I feel. I feel the turbulence. I feel the joy. I feel the fear – oh no!! Please don't land there!!   And I feel the relief – phew, carried up again.

Then I realize I just want to fly. Fly. Fly. I feel like I spent too much time grounded and I simply want to enjoy the experience of being caught in the wind. But the more I fly, the more places and potentials I see. Like a huge smorgasbord of gorgeous possibilities and flavours and experiences. And an old part of me gets angry that so many people schooled me away; that I did – but no more because I am free. Because I embrace me. Because I want my Inner Dandelion to thrive and seed.

The question remains – where will the seeds land? Where do I want them to land? For now they've landed in Cuba so I can feel and experience life-work harmony. That is what I want, life-work harmony. That is what I will patiently and joyously seed and flower for.

Keith Inman

Jungle Resort

A pipe jolted. Light framed the curtains. Monique,
Sheba'd in towels, crossed the room
and stood beside the chair in the corner.
"Dhere is a cricket in our room," she said, staring
at the space above her night stand. Robert spied
the said cricket: long, wide, flat. "Don't think
that's a cricket, hon." He threw back the covers, swung
his pale veined legs out and picked up his sneaker.
Monique, seventy-four, leapt onto the chair. The smack
triggered a sharp rap on the neighbouring
wall as the cockroach fell to the floor. Monique
stood statued, pointing under the bed.

Ten minutes passed, the roach and Robert
playing hide 'n' seek. Beds were moved. Tables
pulled from walls, each scrape accented
by banging above, below, and on all sides.
Robert took a moment and leaned on the bed.
The roach was behind the leg. Monique
whispered to Robert, "Watch your 'eart, dear." Robert
more worried about his knee giving out, gazed
at the roach looking so fresh, its antennae waving
toward him. Robert placed both knees against
the bed and shoved, full on. The roach, pinned,
twisted, then took off limping as the walls
pounded. Monique piped up from her dais,
"Watch your blood, dear." Robert, panting, spied
the roach heading for the door. Somewhat
defeated, he blocked any retreat back
into the room, his leg throbbing, the roach's leg
trailing as it skimmed under the door into the bright
noise of clinking dishes from Juan's Jungle Cafe.
But a shadow remained. The roach wavered
on the threshold of light. 'Go,' Robert thought,
'go, you're free!' But the roach turned
and gimped straight toward the size 11 shoe
in his hand as Liberty screamed, "Get 'Im!"

Richard M. Grove

Digame, Talk to Me

I woke to a humming-jungle-view this morning
strolled down the path to the sleeping pool
sat in the milky-morning haze.
All was quiet and calm. A benevolent breeze
whispered through fluttering palms
like a teenage girl's hip-swaying skirt.
The waking valley flowed
over me like a cathedral brimming
with Gregorian chant.

I basked in peace for over an hour
and then in shock I was pulled
back to earth by the energetic whine
of a cell phone ringing.
A young Cuban woman quickly
shuffled in her deep purse
pulled out her gleaming Samsung Galaxy II
stroked its glowing face and said,
as if talking over droning traffic,
"Digame, Talk to me."
A sharp laugh and chatter rattled
through quivering palms in waking yawn.
My hip swaying Cuban morning interloper
cackled her way out of sight
ducking low drooping branches.

John B. Lee

Broken Money "Bozuk Para"

if you live
in a land
of broken money, lost then
even
in a golden hour
of luminous darkness

under a white shard
of a sand dollar moon

that and
whatever chalkstone
crescent over Cuba
whatever milk-shell
fragment standing there
on the sea draw
of a great shallowing
a grand outwash
of a deepening elsewhere
feeling only that lonesome boatswell
of the heart's inhale
that undulant influence of mutable tides
at the soul of the ocean's imago
over fathomless trenches
where waves rise and fall and fall and rise
form and unform in foam flight
where luxuriant phosphorescent creatures dwell
alive in ultra-white ghost beds
of a great crush

if you measure then
with the sock weight of change
a fool's weapon
or a fortunate jangle of pocket-slung wealth

my father
dancing his hand
in dimes of distraction

someone counting out
the day
by the hen's worth

someone chumming the street
where poverty
scrambles for silver grain
like thirsting in new-fallen rain

if I am ever ungrateful
for the fat profile
of a small copper-faced man

or if I with
the cruel panjandrum
of a single bankable tyrant's jaw
and beard
some much-minted barbarian
seem disgruntled or am fraught by despair
or if it is my luck
to hold true
the fortunate currency of the heart
where I may be blessed by
the bent light
that suffers along the palm line
to the blue regions
of a better place than here

I am perhaps become a prism then
where every dolor
is always a counting house
and every coin
a micromeasure
of a gathering backwards
both from sorrowful exaltation
and joyful sob

Gary Rasberry

Tourist Trap

1. By Day (Taking the Bait)

By day we are all more than happy
to accept the conditions:
welcoming waves white sand blue ocean yellow sun.

Pleasant music playing somewhere.
A soundtrack made to measure.
The length of each day spent
seeking the right amount of pleasure:
Food. Drink. Drink Food. Food Drink.

According to plan we took the bait—
happily unaware. Loving the hand
that fed us. Taking it all
for granted.

By day we were all more than happy.
We knew it was a trap but walked in
willingly. Smiling 'till our teeth hurt.

Feeling eager and deserving.
The ocean our playground
as outlined in the brochure.

None of us had read the fine print
or noticed that 'tourist' and 'trap'
were used in the same sentence.
More than happy. Music and waves.
Loving the soundtrack. White sand.
Smiling food and drinks. Taking it all in.
Taking it all.

The ocean so blue. So big. So blue.
We see it. Feel it. Know it's there for us.
By day we were all more than   happy.

2. By Night (It's later than you think)

The ocean is black. Voices drift
up from the bar. The ocean is
black and only I know it's out there

Beyond the cigarettes and
sickly-sweet rum punches.
Drink up happy tourists.

It's best to inoculate ourselves against this thing
we can not see: the ocean is black.

Sunsets are for postcards and travel brochures only
and right now it's best to aim for oblivion.
Get good and wasted—make sure
we prepare ourselves fully to not feel the bottom

Of a body that knows nothing but the worst
of our fears. Drink up strangers.
Until your lungs no longer care for breath.

Raw meat is the best measure of our worth.
Shark bait a good bet. Smash your glass
against every meager thought that keeps you
afloat.

No one will be dragging for bodies.
In fact, the story you're trying to keep
afloat is a joke about to be told.

Death. No dreaming. Drink up
everyone. None of this means anything
more than the time it takes to realize
there's no bottom.

3. By Day (Redemption still possible)

Next morning there is just one left
to bear witness to the beautiful explosion
of light. The first moments

in which the ocean permits colour
to be reassigned. A brilliant argument
of blue and green along one thin line
of white foam just off shore.

So of course we were all wrong the night before but
too drunk and too touristed to admit it. Black: the ocean
was black. Yes. And we were and are entitled fools.

Reckless and short-sighted. More than willing
to trample one another for blindness
or another drink. But that was then.

Welcome friends. Welcome the Brilliance of Blue.
The aqua genius of sea-green and a palette large enough
for sunrise where oil and watercolour *do* mix.

Maybe we can still be awake in the dreaming.
Realize it's a trap and acknowledge our true captors.
Of course it's a trap. Blue or
black. The ocean doesn't need us. God
spit on our eyes so we can see.

Theodore Christou

I found myself
in some place, abroad

I walk alone on streets I
Know and recognize
No one   nor does anyone recognize
Me   nor truthfully do I feel
Familiar to this
Street   this inanimate
Thing that bustles as if it were more a current
Than a pond

I walk
And look at people
Who walk like
Me and are thinking
Whatever it is that
People think on
Streets and each
Face or manner of dress
Reveals a memory of
Another person I have
Seen on this
Or on another street
In some time past
But each is unrecognizable
And foreign   as I must
Be foreign and indistinct
No sooner seen than
Forgotten   no sooner passed
Pursued or followed
Than transmuted to a cloud
Or shadow that is
Screen to fleeting
Lost imaginings

John B. Lee

El Hombre con La Guitarra Azul

the man with the blue guitar
sings Martí
as we ride
the jaunting cart
horse-drawn along the sea-lit
lanes of Gibara, solo voce
"yo soy un hombre sincero"

and with wife
and friends in chorus
the song
in harmony lifting
over the buzz of shining strings
the melodious
mourning of the recent loss
of America's quintessential troubadour
of peace and source of song

that sky we see
is also star-subsuming blue
and this Jorge
with whom we share
a brilliant ear
one hour
in the cool grotto
a common cave
like the mind of the earth

two rock climbers
spider the wall
with handgrip and toehold
and float rope
and hang cradle

while three guitars
one mandolin
and twelve voices
flicker the candle of a distant room
as it is with the echolalia
of a much-remembered day

the priestly sigh at the end of service
the poet
breathless at the end of an overlong line
the lover
in pleasure, the child
in grief
and the eidelon of memory
saying hello and again hello

John B.Lee

Forgetful

here within this sand-white arc
of bent bones long-lost in the disinterment of a deep grave
at the sad moment
when the heart drops through
as on some archeological
grey-water gloaming
when heaven refuses the light loss
as it is with autumn's over-ripening
some winter orchard's
lassitude for the outlasting of medlars
this woman
in her island cerements
her skull bejeweled by a sacred stone
her forehead turned
to her mate
giving the halo-gaze
of love, the one she gave in life
the selfsame devotion, the quickening
that dimples the blue pulse points inspiring
the language of desire
how is it
that this pre-Columbian princess
has come to dust through dust
with this intact sombrelito
this capshadow of the soul
this small darkness
she holds
as a child might close
a half shell in her hand
the one she will find in the morning
and lose in the evening
forgetful of grieving

Richard M. Grove

Morning Light

A calm soughing
from her side of the bed,
an angel purrs
in the whisper-hour
of sunrise.
Mi esposa's hand
like a soft linen napkin draped
over the edge of a table
wedding ring glistens
in curtained thin-morning light.

I gently click the door closed
behind me and quietly drift
down the path to the silence
of a cloud-roofed room
with the palm-swaying
mist-filled view
of our waking valley.

The ghost of a thrubbing bird
echoes in timeless jungle.

A distant oxen mournfully moos
to the shadow-less dawn.

Cynthia Mitchell

The Price
for Pablo

I hope you do not lose
the feeling you have
the connection to environment
the connection to family
the connection to something more
          the peace of spirituality

Because what the rest of the world has
what the rest of the world sells
doesn't bring happiness
truthfully it brings pain
          because it costs the spirit

Yes it helps
          without a doubt
to make
          things
          easier

But the truth
     is that it comes with a price
          too high

When you want things
Ask yourself:
          What is the price
               of the Soul?

John B. Lee

One Morning in Mayabe

in the morning in Mayabe
a lone vulture
soars, kiting the thermals
the black flag
of his dropshadow
drifting echo-darkness over the mango groves
caressing the orchards by the lake
as though with the sorrowful breath
of a widow's veil—
we walk the hill
through medlar and soursop
the long leathering pods
of the flamboyant
rattling their saber sheathes
over the shortswords
of a wind on the march
as up we rise
along the donkey-dung road
to the finca casa of a reconstructed farm
there in the burnt-bean gloom
of a Cuban kitchen
Wency is doing the coffee dance
with mortar and pestle
and I am reminded how it was for me
making butter, churning in the milk slosh
of my own childhood home
as with the ache in my small boy arms
I felt myself
a drudge of the slow globulation
plunging the weight of a wooden cross
in turbulent oleaginous coagulation
of ultra-yellow coldering
clatter, listing that stick from the suck
like curding and cheese clabber

what was that then
but the seemingly endless ennui
of a child's labour
and my mother
in time, gone butter black
a glossy tabula rasa
and I'm
a drone of dead roses
my heart
the stone of a busy hill

Keith Inman

Escher's Stairs, Cuba
after a Tai, CCLA, Joseph Campbell, exercise

We woke to another blue sky of t-shirt
heat and walked upstairs to breakfast.
I was amazed how many people had
already claimed pool chairs. We
took the back stairs down, and found
slight nuances of what had been yesterday
and what was now today, here a cloud,
there a breeze tugging the paint peeled
red and white facade of tourist block,
and the rough sea beyond, breaking low
over a pier that had survived a hurricane,
stones still out of place along a hibiscus
perfumed promenade, boats trained
to the dock with the days catch, the best

known whitefish around. The same worker
from Karaoke night swept palm debris.
He suggested we try downstairs for lunch.
We had burgers, scurried back like crabs
in the noon light when ocean currents
turned green under the sun. There were slight
nuances between what had been the day
before and what were higher waves
on the beach, the tide's turquoise
river rippling shallow sandbars and
a bartender's smile one day further
into serving this week's drunks, tattooed
punks for example their junk hanged out,
never leaving the chlorined pool, drink

after drink, the volley ball never sinking,
the sun beating red and redder.
The steps to evening were well lit.
Above and beyond all this, we'd booked
the best restaurant within the compound,
yet waited for waiters on home-turf-
time. But the wine was fine. We tipped
a sand dollar, strolled part of the complex
we'd never been to before and stared up
at a revolution of stars beyond the rain
threatened wind tinkling with tree frogs
singing in the half-bottle night. We waited
for the moon to rise, but it is not out there
anywhere beyond the cracked balustrades.

Theodore Christou

pilgrim

crawl with me love, to the sea;

to sunny, swept waters; to laughter; to music and song.

we will sing songs of rancor to conjure the black; to
draw forth the shadows that burden our backs.

the sea and the sun will swallow the pains; and our
sorrow and hate. and our laughter and song.

into the sea, serenely, we'll slip.

John B. Lee

On the Beauty of Being Elsewhere

I look out through
window glaze freshly frosted in last-night's snow
like the clinging there of new-washed linen
and beyond that glimpse
the sublimation of bushes
those fine-boned creatures
purified by winter
even where wind song
seems at this white hour
in the burning cold
overfull with sunlight calcified
like chalkstone—oh my Ontario morning
I am saying farewell
as I'm rising in the belly of this silver bird
emerging into a post-prandial blue
walking the humid torpor
of a Cuban evening
feeling the lovely melancholia
of being elsewhere

like a rose of ice
I water away
una rosa blanca
dying in the crystalline wave
Irish linen grown old
a snowflake on the tongue
of a child reciting Martí
amused by a poem he knows
as he knows in a moment
of ice and water
and water and sky's blue aspic
concealing the invisible flavour of light

Gary Rasberry

When God Was a Boy
for Pablo

Then we met The Boy from Holguin
and we saw The Light. We knew
right then and there:

We were in the Presence of   God.
Perhaps we should not have been so surprised
by his age? God was 9 years old.

Still we had no cause for doubt.
After all—just under a decade
on this Earthly Plain is surely long enough

to get a good sense of how much Work there is
to be done here. Yes it made sense that God
was so young: The Holy Spirit

with a lovely crooked grin and beautiful brown eyes
that saw us so clearly. Inside and out. He loved us
for our flaws and imperfections. Loved us

for the goodness He knew we were capable of.
Yes, it was a blessed relief that God was so young.

One smile from Him and we knew Everything was possible.
His smile was always enough, yes, but there were also
his short stories, funny jokes, earnest parables, playful
sermons, a pointed narrative added for good measure.

Our hearts burned brighter
for those moments basking in a
Light of the most astonishing
quality. There may have been some

who thought it was just the Cuban sun:
the fanciful play of light and leaf and limb.
But the rest of us knew beyond a shadow:

God was a boy. What else was there to do
but offer up our poems and prayers
and wait for the healing.

Richard M. Grove

Burial Ground Visit

we are tourists
gawking
staring at eternity
yesterday's lives
yesterday's loves
today's dust
carved in time
now simply a different
molecular structure
entombed
in camera flashes

Keith Inman

Ground
Ancient Burial Site, Cuba

The land looks older than the book says.
Could be this worried scrag
vegetation under a hard sun.
A man carrying his weight of stone
up a sinewed path of red rock passes
our big blue bus parked on the back
of the mountain. There is a museum
we are to see, an ancient cemetery
of southern migrants from the main-
land a thousand years ago.

Piles of bleached bones on dirt pedestals
crowd the sunken site. A chieftain, the curator
points, interred with colourful pebbles placed
on his breast. His wife at rest beside him. Farther
over, a child, appears to have
gone to sleep. And bundled apart, there
in the far corner upside
down, a folded nest of a man. "A bad
man," says the curator. "Notice the position
of the burial. West African. You can tell
by the shape of his bones." "What
did he do wrong?" a flowered tourist asks.
"We don't know, of course," says the curator.

The bus bumps back to town busy
with dust driven trucks full of dark,
ball-capped men, bright families
in speeding Ladas, plaid-shirted farmers
reining their horse-drawn buggies, goods
wrapped under blankets, pale uniformed boys
on motor bikes, sun-kissed girls, skirted
on low pedal bikes, a kerchiefed white
women stirring a pot on the porch while yelling
at an old black man, who ignores her as he plays
dominoes, the bare unpainted houses
the colour of ground.

John B. Lee

The Ungoable

it was the opposite of falling—
seeing her mother
waving from the shore
as she and her sisters
stood at the railing
of the ship
leaving Europe
after the war
her mother dimming
to a sorrowful deflation
a reified vanishment of love breaking the heart
the way the crag of a cove
breaks a wave
at the thin edge of the sea
one high sharp
exhilarating shatter-glass
moment of roaring
and sumping the rock hollows
to feel that unswallowable grief
the herniated ache
at the hiatus of an inheld sob
surely only a child
can hurt that way
yet I see
in the telling
how this lovely woman
relives the deep throb of loss
revivifying for the fraulein she was
born in Berlin
before the conflagration of the city
with its fire dead
immolated in the burning strausses
the Fuhrer sneering
through flame flowers
rising from the red garlands of his bones

the Swastika
blasted by sappers
crashing to the earth

lightning in the high branches
and the eagle kinder
of the Phoenix with no future

she mentions
a certain officer of the conquering Soviet
lusting after her mother
who was beautiful
and when her mother refused
his unwanted advances
he lined up her five children
placed a loaded pistol to each
of their temples
touching the muzzle
to the pulse point of each young mind
that black zero's cold metallic kiss
and then firing a single shot
in the air at the end, so she knew
the inescapable consequence
of a mother's refusal

and the same dignified
and much-loved mother
violated by the cruelty
of a choice
that is no choice

stood on the pier at the shore of the harbour
waving
he hand like the last glimpse
of the desperate drowned

those who are helpless in history
because they know
by the needle of some inner compass
the ungoable direction of hope

In Memoriam:

Editor's note: Brian Mullally and I had communicated early with his work contained within this anthology. He was very happy to have been included, and was looking forward to seeing the completed anthology. I was very saddened to learn of his death, a few days after a final email to him went unanswered. Out of my deepest sympathy for his family, his wife Maureen and his many friends, I found it fitting to include this memorial page to him. My thanks to Guy Mullally, his son, for composing the short eulogy below and for including one of Brian's own favourite poems.

Brian Terence Mullally
(February 27, 1929 – July 18, 2015)

Brian was born in Croydon, England on February 27, 1929. Six months later the stock market crashed and the world was plunged into the Great Depression, followed closely by World War II. It was a difficult time to grow up in and it left an indelible impression. Too young to fight in the war, Brian joined the airways in 1948 and saw what war had done to world – the destruction, the rebuilding and the hope. In 1954, Brian came to Canada with his beloved wife Maureen, ten dollars in his pocket and a book: "Five Acres and Independence". Brian and Maureen had five children and Brian worked at many different jobs – from labourer to factory worker, salesman to entrepreneur – to provide something for his family that he never had – security, safety – a magical place called home where anything was possible and life was a big adventure.

The years went by, as they do. In 1992, Brian and Maureen built a small bungalow on a large treed lot in a new development on the outskirts of Cobourg, Ontario and Brian began to do what he had always wanted to do; what he was very probably born to do. He started writing – and once he started he couldn't stop. He had so many stories to tell, so many anecdotes and poignant moments, an incredible treasure trove of memories and experiences to share. In all he wrote three books, published two, as well as a book of short stories and contributions to three other anthologies of short stories; not to mention the dozens of stories and the autobiography he was working on when he left his desk. Brian's work reveals his compassion, his sense of humour and his gentle understanding of human nature. It is as vivid, entertaining and alive as he was and will remain for all who read it.

Brian Mullally, writer, salesman, entrepreneur; son, brother, lover, husband, father, grandfather, great grandfather; a daring adventurer who took risks and defied odds, who travelled the world on a cork, built castles for his family, who always saw the best in people, always saw the sunshine peeking through on a cloudy day; a man who loved life and lived a life of joy and optimism.

ALIEN FLOWER

Standing tall in summer grasses
In the last damp days of June
Still the memory never passes
Violet blue they're now in bloom
In the last damp days of June
Like they looked the day we met
Violet blue they are now in bloom
Precious eyes I can't forget
Like they looked the day we met
Viper's Bugloss. What a shame!
Precious eyes I can't forget
Who gave this plant its nasty name?
Alien flowers of gorgeous hue
Still the memory never passes
Like the girl with eyes so blue
Standing tall in summer grasses

Brian Mullally

Acknowledgements

Deborah Panko – "Meditation on Occupy Wall Street" , "Northumberland's Highway of Heroes" and "In Late Afternoon" were all previously published in Blueprint, (Crow-Magnon, 2014).

Donna Langevin –Poems found in this anthology have also appeared in her chapbook, The Middle-Aged Man in the Sea, (Lyrical Miracle Press, 2009).

James Cockcroft -- His poem in this anthology comes from the expanded second edition of his book "Why? ¿Por Qué? Pourquoi?" [Hidden Brook Press, 2nd ed., 2012].

K.V. Skene – "Miles" was published in an anthology, Listening to the Birth of Crystals, 2004
"Where Sea Ends" was published by Reach Poetry 117, December 2007
"No Matter What Sun Warms" was published by Reach Poetry 151, April 2011

Lisa Makarchuk— All poems appearing in this anthology were previously published in the '1st Anthology of the International Festival of Poetry of Resistance (IFPOR)'.

Patrick Connors –"Somewhere Down the Zen River" has been posted on the blogs of Chris Faiers and Anna Yin.

Author Bios:

Adela González-Longoria Escalona was born in Gibara on June 9th, 1951. She is a housewife and a poet. Adela is a member of the literary workshops 'Armando Leyva 'and 'Fernándo Cuesta'. She has received awards and recognition from a variety of contests and events in the Gibara municipality. She is a member of the 'CCLA Sea Dreamers', a writer's group in Gibara.

 Adislenis Castro Ruiz, an engineer, lives in Gibara, Holguín, Cuba, born in 1972. She is a poet and narrator, and a member of the Municipal Literary Workshop (Armando Leyva Balaguer) and the Literary Workshop (Manuel Armando Gómez Fernández). Her works have been published in the bulletins 'Cacoyugüin' (of the system de Casas de Cultura), and in 'Arrecife' (from the municipal bookstore of Gibara). Her work has also appeared on the web page 'El Pescador de Orilla' (the municipal library of Gibara). Her literary creations have been revealed in the cultural institutions of her village, and she has received awards and references for her work in municipal competitions.

Adonay B. Pérez Luengo is a professor at the University of Pedagogical Sciences "José de la Luz y Caballero", Holguín, Cuba. She has a Bachelor Degree in Geography, and a Masters in The Sciences of Education. She combines her passion for teaching with her love for poetry. Adonay is a member of the CCLA. She is also the reviewer of the Spanish texts published by Hidden Brook Press (HBP) and Sand Crab Books (SCB). Several of her poems have been published by the CCLA.

Brian Gordon Sinclair, B.A., B.Ed., M.A. – director, performer and playwright – is a graduate of the National Theatre School of Canada. He has also studied at the Royal Academy of Dramatic Arts in London, England and at the National Film Board of Canada.

Mr. Sinclair is the author of *The Hemingway Monologues: An Epic Drama of Love, Genius and Eternity*, a seven volume series detailing the life and literature of Ernest Hemingway. Other publications include *Cuba Solidarity in Canada* (Chapter 12), *The Homerun Kid: The True Story of Ernest Hemingway's Baseball Team* and *Easter Rising: The Last Words of Patrick Pearse*, a recreation of the 1916 struggle for freedom in Dublin, Ireland. He is considered to be the "foremost dramatic interpreter of Ernest Hemingway in the world." (Stratford-upon-Avon Herald, UK)

Brian Mullally (1929-2015) is the author of several novels, most notably *Make Me an Offer* (2006) and *If I Were a Blackbird* (2010) and well over a hundred short stories. He has won five awards for his short fiction and the wide range of his work is displayed in his collection of twenty stories, *A Patch of Blue* (2011).

Rooted in Northumberland where he lived with his wife and family for nearly 50 years, he made a significant contribution to the writing community in his area. Recent publications are to be found in *Hill Spirits, An Anthology by Writers from Northumberland County,* Vols. 1 and 2, (2012 and 2015). He will be much missed.

Chris Faiers received the first Milton Acorn People's Poet Medal in 1987. 19 collections of his work have been published, and his poetry has appeared in well over 100 mags, anthologies and scholarly publications. Among his literary contributions are founding The Main Street Library Poetry Series and Unfinished Monument Press. He is an honorary lifetime member of the Canada-Cuba Literary Alliance. A retired village librarian, Chris coordinates annual Purdy Country Literary Festivals, and enjoys stewarding his Zen River Gardens retreat.

Cynthia Mitchell through 'Sweet Perspectives' offers a fresh new outlook on life! As a life coach, Cynthia empowers people to live their dreams, love who they are, and make positive change in themselves and the world. As a writer, Cynthia helps people present their authentic self on the written page. As a motivator, Cynthia inspires people to believe in who they are by re-writing old beliefs, re-wiring old thoughts, and re-connecting passion. As an educator, Cynthia focuses on teaching the how parts of positive change. Cynthia is currently working on her manuscript "The Beauty of Disaster," a book to inspire compassionate people to live their passions, usurp their bullies, take leadership positions, and make positive change.

Danielle Dinally is a writer of fiction and poetry and she aspires to become better at her craft every day. She has recently completed her studies and graduated with a BA in Creative Writing and Literature at York University in October 2014. She writes for online publications such as FanFiction, Booksie, Scribd, and is currently the editor of the Envoy, the official newsletter of the CCLA. Her latest project is a novella based on a troubled youth from Canada who must stay and do community service in Cuba after blinding a Cuban officer. The novella still remains title-less and has been inspired by Cuba itself as a country and its wonderful people.

Deborah Panko lives in Cobourg, ON having retired from teaching English in Toronto. Hidden Brook Press published her first book of poetry, *Somewhat Elsewhere* in 2008, and *From O to Snow* with Kate Marshall-Flaherty and Donna Langevin in 2010. *Photograph-Do Not Bend/Poems Not for Pretend* is a tribute to her late husband, Ron Cole, a photographer who traveled widely over many decades (Crow-Magnon Publishing, 2013) followed by her most recent book of poems, *Blueprint* (Crow-Magnon Publishing, 2014).

Donna Langevin's latest poetry collections include *In the Café du Monde*, Hidden Brook Press *2008,* and *The Laundress of Time,* Aeolus Press *2015*. She won first prize in the TOPS Contest 2008 and also in the Cyclamens and Swords contest 2009. She was short-listed for the Descant 2010 Winston Collins prize and won second prize in the GritLIT Poetry Competition 2014.

About Donna's plays: *The Man with a Butterfly Hat* was produced at the Toronto Alumnae Theatre for NIF, 2012. *Welcome to Nuit Blanche* was produced at the Ryerson 50+ Festival 2014. *The Dinner* won first prize in the one act play contest for the Eden Mills Writers' Festival 2014.

Ernesto Galbán Peramo: Gibara,1965. He received his B. A. in Art History from the University of Oriente in 1988 and his Masters Degree in the same field from the University of Havana in 2004. He teachers at the University of Pedagogical Sciences in Holguín. He has received several awards in poetry contests in his hometown.

He has participated in many national and international literary events, has also written several fine arts exhibit catalogues, as well as the forewords to books on music and fine arts. Some of his poems have been published in The Ambassador.

Gary Rasberry. Philosopher. Poet. *Imagination Consultant.* Musician. Artist. Educator. Insecure Extrovert. Reluctant Enthusiast. Small Animal with Fast Metabolism. 'More Naked Than Ever' is his latest book of espresso-based poems. Gary is in the studio recording his next album, 'The Very Next Day' and has toured with The Big Idea Band doing shows for his JUNO-nominated record, 'What's the Big Idea?!?' Gary's time in Cuba with the CCLA was a rich and beautiful experience. He found poetry everywhere—in the places and in the people.

George Arnold currently serves as president of the Inkwell Writers Group. He is the author of 2 well received books of poetry and is a popular reader at poetry events across Ontario. He has also been published in a variety of newspapers, magazines, and anthologies. George resides in a peaceful corner of Oakville, Ontario with his beloved wife and youngest daughter. He delights in enabling other poets, especially the young poets of tomorrow.

Heide Brown's first memory of writing with joy is when she was 11, and writing and producing plays for her Girl Guide friends. Since that time she has filled her file-cabinet with multiple drafts of stories, memoirs and poems, and filled her bookshelf with journals.

Since 1990 she has lived on Gabriola Island, B.C. She loves this place almost as much as she loves writing, painting, hooking rag-rugs and sharing her life with family, friends, and The Gabriola Commons, which she co-founded.

Hugh Hazelton is a writer and translator who lives in Montreal. His third book of poetry, *Antimatter*, was reprinted with CD by Broken Jaw Press in 2010; a Spanish version came out with Split Quotation/La Cita Trunca in 2009. He performs his poems in several languages and believes that poetry should bite, caress, stroke, laugh at, confront, lament, name, imagine, envision, remember, invoke, oppose, and reflect.

James Cockcroft - As an award-winning author of 50 books, James has published poetry in sundry anthologies. He is Honorary Editor of *Latin American Perspectives*; a founder of the Red en Defensa de la Humanidad; and a member of the UNESCO-sponsored Consejo Mundial del Proyecto José Martí de Solidaridad Internacional. His latest books are: "WHY? ¿POR QUÉ? POURQUOI? POETRY & POESÍA" (Hidden Brook Press, second expanded edition 2012) and "MEXICO'S REVOLUTION THEN AND NOW" (NY: Monthly Review Press, 2010, also in 2 Spanish editions & 2 French editions). www.jamescockcroft.com

James Deahl was born in 1945. He lives in Sarnia with the writer Norma West Linder. He is the author of twenty-three literary titles, the four most recent being: *Two Paths Through The Seasons* (with Norma West Linder, 2014), *North Point* (2012), *Rooms The Wind Makes* (2012), and *North Of Belleville* (with Richard M. Grove, 2012). He is the father of Sarah, Simone, and Shona.

John Hamley used to be a fisheries scientist and computer salesman, but then he retired and with his brother built a house in the woods of eastern Ontario, where they now live with the trees and the "beasties."

John B. Lee is a member in good standing of the CCLA and a frequent traveler in Cuba. His two collections inspired by Cuba are *Island on the Wind Breathed Edge of the Sea*, and *In This We Hear the Light*. In 2010 in collaboration with friend Dr. Manuel de Jesus Velazquez Leon, his co-translation of Cuban poetry *Sweet Cuba: The Building of a Poetic Tradition 1608-1958* was published by Hidden Brook Press. Called 'the most significant book of translated Cuban poetry ever published," Mr. Lee remains very proud of his special relationship with Cuban poetry. John B. Lee is the only Poet Laureate of two communities in Canada. He is Poet Laureate of the city of Brantford in perpetuity and Poet Laureate of Norfolk County for life. He lives in a lake house overlooking Long Point Bay on Lake Erie in Port Dover.

Jorge Alberto Pérez Hernández was born in Santiago de Cuba in 1961 and now resides in Gibara. He has a Bachelor of Arts degree in English Language, was a university Professor, and taught for thirty years at a number of educational levels. He worked as a coordinator at the National Institute of Tourism Hotel "Sierra Maestra" of Bayamo, belongs to the literary workshop 'Creators Peña Gibara, and his work has been published in literary newsletters 'Reef', 'Villa Blanca' and 'The Envoy'.

He has participated in the teaching and learning workshop of foreign languages, ENALEX, and after investigative work received his diploma. He has participated in national and international events related to his profession. He received mention in a local literary competition, genre 'Armando Leyva Poetry', during the 'Day of Culture' in the town of San Fulgencio de Gibara.

M. Pérez is a member of the Canada Cuba Literary Alliance and holds the title of Ambassador. He is the founding president of the CCLA, Gibara writers group called the "Sea Dreamers" and coordinated their first anthology entitled *Marea de sueños: Selección de poesía* (ISBN - 978-1-927725-01-6).

June Salmon's eclectic lifestyle and view of the world colour her poetry, and in it she hopes will strike a chord with readers and inspire hope and love of life.

K.V. Skene's publications include *Love in the (Irrational) Imperfect*, (Hidden Brook Press, Canada ,2006) and *You Can Almost Hear Their Voices*, (Indigo Dreams Publishing, UK, 2010). Her poetry sequence, "The Whitening of the Ox", originally published in Descant in 1996, was set to music by Jeffrey Ryan, and presented in January 2012 at Toronto's Harbourfront and in August 2012 at Vancouver's MusicFest. After living for over eighteen years in the UK and Ireland, she repatriated herself and is currently living in Toronto, Canada.

Katharine Beeman is a Montreal poet involved in international solidarity, and with writers and artists encouraging cultural creation as indispensable to understanding and changing the world. She has five published poetry collections and many poems in reviews and anthologies. She participates avidly in Festivals and readings anywhere she can get to.

Keith Inman's work can be found in *Window Fishing: The night we caught Beatlemania* from Hidden Brook Press and *An Unfinished War* from Black Moss Press, books edited by John B. Lee. Other sources that have shared his work are *Descant, CV2, The New Quarterly, Event, and Studies: An Irish Review*. He has had the honour of receiving a few Ontario Arts Council grants, has had two chapbooks published and a first full length book of poetry *The War Poems: Screaming at Heaven*, about the human condition at home during Canada's War years, due out this fall from Black Moss Press. Keith lives in Thorold, Ontario.

Kimberley Grove has taught creative writing at Loyalist College, Universidad of Ciego de Avila in Cuba, the Colborne Community Care, and from her home. She has been published in the *Christian Science Monitor*, *The Globe and Mail*, *The Toronto Star, the Boston Globe,* and other local publications. She has worked as a staff and freelance journalist. Her book *Stories Inked* was a commissioned manuscript for ORT Toronto. Her book *Family Ties*, an international anthology of family short stories was published in 2014.

Lisa Makarchuk worked in radio in Cuba during the sixties and ever since has been involved in solidarity movements. Starting with solidarity in the plight of political prisoners imprisoned by Salazar in Portugal and Franco in Spain, helping to organize the Hemispheric Conference Against the Viet Nam War, acting in defense of self-determination and sovereignty of Cuba and freedom for the Cuban Five, she co-founded the International Festival of Poetry of Resistance in 2009. She is currently in the process of being published in a collection of essays on the Canada-Cuba solidarity movement.

Manuel de Jesús Velázquez León is a professor of studies of the English-speaking cultures of the University of Holguín. He does research and writes on British, Canadian and American cultures as well as on moral education. His literary activities include translation as well as short story and poetry writing. Manuel is the VP of the Canada Cuba Literary Alliance and the Editor-in-chief of *The Ambassador* magazine. He is also the publisher of SandCrab Books, a subsidiary of Hidden Brook Press.

Merle Hernández González says of her poems in this anthology, "These poems were written thinking about a person closer to me, she is alive, but I think the poems could be for others who feel identified with them. 'Saint Love' speaks of all virtues that every people must get in their life, for being happy or living well in harmony. It is the invitation to change, to the conversion to be a better person. I write some words in capital for highlighting the actions or virtues. 'Stony Heart' is an invocation to change too, the way of thinking, and acting in a good mood, but in this case, I felt a disappointment with her actions to others and I wanted to transmit this sense to the readers in these lines".

Miriam Estrella Vera Delgado Miriam Estrella Vera Delgado was born in Holguin, Cub. She was a Ship Invoicer in Moa Harbor for 23 year, and a private English teacher for 10. She began writing stories in the 90's and received several awards in literary contests. Her publishing and writing history includes - a story in English 'The Burnt Tower' (2004), and began writing poetry in Spanish (2005) then in English (2008).

Her poetry was featured in an issue of "Stellar Showcase Journal" (2009

Spring), and her story 'Paranormal Phenomena in my Life' was serialized in the same journal. Her book of poetry, *From the Heart*, was published by J. Graham Publishing (Canada, 2010). Also in Dec. of that year her poems were published in the literary magazine "The Ambassador", and in "The Secret Silence of the Valley" – a bilingual anthology of poets from Holguín. In 2011, her poems were included in the English anthology "When the Full Moon Comes", and several poems were published in the bilingual anthology "Taste of the Rainbow" (2012). Her poetry has been included in "The Ambassador Volume 12", and her poems and short stories have been frequently featured in 'The Envoy'. In October 2014, several of her poems were published in a Nostre Club anthology in Barcelona, Spain.

Patrick Connors has been published in Zouch Magazine & Miscellany, This Place Anthology, Northern Voices Journal, Poetry'Z Own Magazine, Chrysalis Zine, and was shortlisted for the 2011 Best of the Net contest. He was Lead Artist in the pilot of 'Making a Living; Making Art', a project of Cultural Pluralism in the Arts at the University of Toronto. He was literary juror of Big Art Book 2013, a digital project of Scarborough Arts. In celebration of National Poetry Month, he was featured on the blogs of The Toronto Quarterly and the League of Canadian Poets. His first chapbook, *Scarborough Songs*, was released by Lyricalmyrical Press in 2013. He has also recently had work published in Belgium, India, and Timmins. He is part of an anthology coming out next February in Cuba, and is also working on a full manuscript. He is a manager for the Toronto chapter of 100,000 Poets for Change.

Paul R. Carr has written and edited several books of poetry, including *My Malecón* (2000), and *Concave mirrors / Espejos concavos* (2013), and has collaborated with Cuban poets for a number of years. He is a Professor of Sociology at the Université du Québec en Outaouais.

Paulos Ioannou is the author of four full-length poetry collections written in Greek. Aeolus House published his first full-length poetry anthology in English "The Age of Hydra" in early 2009. "The Age of Hydra" was translated into Spanish. He lives in Toronto and was the Chair of the Planning Group for the International Day of People With Disabilities from 2005 to 2010 organized on behalf of the City of Toronto in support of the United Nations' International Day of Persons with Disabilities. He is the editor of the "Monday Nights at Butler's Pantry" anthology featuring four poets: Honey Novick, Naomi Hendrickje Laufer, Don Stabler and Joan Sutcliffe. His latest poetry anthology "The Torontonians, the good, the bad and the other" published by CAN/CYP publications in July 2010 is dedicated to Toronto and each section portrays a facet of that city.

Raúl Vera Delgado was born in Holguín, Cuba. He works as an informatics specialist and lives in Havana. He has been writing poetry since 2011 and a couple of his poems have been published in the Ambassador and The Envoy. Email address: raulvera60@gmail.com.

Raymond Fenech embarked on his writing career at 18, freelancing for three Maltese political newspapers and working as a journalist with *The Times of Malta*. He edited two nation-wide distributed magazines, and has published his work in 12 countries. He is a creative writing professor with a UK based online university and a writing therapist. His research on Maltese ghosts appeared in *The International Directory of the Most Haunted Places by Penguin Books*, USA. The author is listed in the International Who's Who in Poetry and Poets" Encyclopaedia, and the Who's Who of Maltese Authors Dictionary.

Richard M. Grove, Hamilton born, lives in Presqu'ile Provincial Park with writer, editor wife, Kim. He is an active photographer/writer/editor/publisher. His art and photographs are in over 30 corporate collections across Canada. He graduated from the Ontario College of Art in 1984. He has 14 book titles to his name and his images have been used as cover art for almost 75 books. He runs Hidden Brook Press and is the founding president of the CCLA – www.Canada Cuba Literary Alliance.org. He was the president of the Canadian Poetry Association, the VP of the Canadian Authors Association Toronto, the founding president of the Brighton Arts Council. You can find his Cuba Blog at http://cubablog.hiddenbrookpress.com/, and Hidden Brook Press at www.HiddenBrookPress.com.

Roger Langen is Irish-French-Maliseet from Perth-Andover, New Brunswick. Educated in Toronto and Newfoundland, he worked as a union executive with the Ontario Secondary School Teachers' Federation, Toronto, before retiring in 2013. He is currently teaching in China and editing a collection of poetry to be entitled, "Imagine Freedom: Power on Trial in the High Court of Poetry".

Shane Joseph is the author of three novels and two collections of short stories. His work *After the Flood* won the best fantasy novel award at the Word Awards in Canada in 2010. His short fiction has appeared in international literary journals and anthologies. His latest story collection, *Paradise Revisited,* was released in the fall of 2013. For details, visit his website at www.shanejoseph.com

Tara Kainer grew up in Knoxville, Tennessee and Regina, Saskatchewan. She attended the University of Regina and Queen's University, Kingston. In 2011 Hidden Brook Press published a book of her poems, *When I Think On Your Lives*. Tara has three grown sons, and currently works in the social justice office of the Sisters of Providence of St. Vincent de Paul.

Theodore Michael Christou is an Associate Professor of Social Studies at Queen's University where he is cross-appointed in Education and in History. He began his academic career at the University of New Brunswick. He is the author of "The Problem of Progressive Education" (University of Toronto Press, 2012), a historical consideration of Ontario's educational history that was awarded the Canadian History of Education Association's Founders Prize for best book in the history of education. He has also authored *an overbearing eye* (Hidden Brook Press, 2013), a book of verse and short fiction.

Wency Rosales - Holguin. Cuba. 1972. Teacher and Translator. CCLA member. His work has been published in different magazines and anthologies. His chapbook " Shades of my Feelings " was also published in Canada in 2008. He works as Entertainer and Public Relations Assistant at Mirador de Mayabe Hotel in Holguin Cuba.

Yanet Alejo Milian was born on July 3rd, 1988 in Ciego de Avila, Cuba. She graduated in English Language and French in 2013. She works as a Translator at the University of Ciego de Avila, and also writes articles for the "El Generalisimo" newspaper. After having written for a number of years, she recently began devoting more time to the craft after taking lessons on writing ('How to Write Short Stories') with the Canadian teacher Kim Grove, and studied poetry with Kim's husband, Richard Grove, President of the Canada Cuba Literary Alliance. Since having become a member of the CCLA, she has sent her work to "The Envoy". It, last July, published three of her poems: 'A Fruity Day', 'City Image' and 'A Harboured Day'. She says she feels like a 'newborn writer' and continues to send poems their way.

Our Editor:

Bruce Kauffman lives in Kingston, Ontario, Canada and is a poet, writer, freelance editor and workshop facilitator. His published work includes a chapbook of poetry, *seed* (The Plowman, 2005), two stand-alone poems: "streets" (Thee Hellbox Press, 2009) and "eulogy" (Puddles of Sky Press, 2015). His work has been published in a number of periodicals and anthologies, and has appeared in three plays. Two of his poems were featured and on display at Kingston Writers Fest 2014's 'Stitch and Stanza', a collaborative effort connecting local fibre artists and poets. He has had three full collections of poetry published: *The Texture of Days, in Leaf and Ash* (Hidden Brook Press, 2013), *a seed within* (Hidden Brook Press, 2013), and *The Silence Before the Whisper Comes* (Hidden Brook Press, 2013).

In 2009 he created and continues to host a monthly open-mic reading series ('and the journey continues'). In 2010, created and also continues to host a weekly spoken word radio show on CFRC 101.9fm in Kingston ('finding a voice'). In 2012, began facilitating 'intuitive writing' workshops. Earlier this month he created and organized a 4-day poetry event, Poets @ Artest, and hopes it will become an annual event. He is the Acquisitions and Poetry Editor for Wintergreen Studios Press, a board member of Queen's Poetry Slam, a Canadian editor for CCLA's *The Ambassador*, and he free-lance edits as well.